PRAYING THE PSALTER

(FOR WOMEN)

DAVID RAPP

WESTBOW
PRESS®
A DIVISION OF THOMAS NELSON
& ZONDERVAN

WestBow Press books may be ordered through booksellers or by contacting:

WestBow Press
A Division of Thomas Nelson & Zondervan
1663 Liberty Drive
Bloomington, IN 47403
www.westbowpress.com
844-714-3454

ISBN: 979-8-3850-1480-4 (sc)
ISBN: 979-8-3850-1481-1 (e)

Library of Congress Control Number: 2023923830

Print information available on the last page.

WestBow Press rev. date: 12/15/2023

INTRODUCTION

As I have always heard and known the Psalms to be "songs of prayer" and recognized the prayerful nature of most of them, I found myself wanting to pray them verbatim, only to feel thwarted routinely because the psalmist would change his audience, from man to God, back and forth, frequently within the same Psalm. A good example of this is found in Psalm 23. It begins by talking *about* God, "The Lord is my shepherd." (verse 1) Then, it is directed *to* God, "You are with me." (verse 4). Then, it concludes by again talking *about* God: "And I will dwell in the house of the Lord forever." (verse 6).

This "problem" created in me a desire to adjust the text so that I could pray it, with all of it directed toward God. In doing so, I quickly discovered that I had to be ok with taking some liberties with the text. My goal was to provide seamless prayers that stay as close to the text of the Psalms as possible, using various versions throughout, to create a flow that I am comfortable with and understand. That is to say, my goal was not to rewrite the Psalms but merely to create prayers that I can read and pray, using words and phrases that I would use, while staying as true to the Psalms as possible.

This led me to the next "problem" I encountered, namely that some Psalms seem largely inapplicable to me today. Some are based on the psalmist's unique experiences, as he recalls specific victories over or deliverance from enemies. With some, he calls on God to destroy his adversaries. Some are written specifically to or about Israel or Jerusalem. And some seem to be merely a message or a history lesson to the reader, more than a prayer to God. Accordingly, after much prayer and careful consideration I took some liberties with the text, using my best effort to maintain the heart of the Scripture, to transform all 150 Psalms into prayers, continually directed *to* God, and adding, at the bottom of each, some attributes of God revealed in the Psalm above.

"Messing" with Scripture caused me to really struggle through the process, taking more than seven years to write this. The following quote from historian, Arnold J. Toynbee, however, encouraged me to finish strong and with confidence, knowing that this cannot be perfect and does not have to be:

"All human work is imperfect, because human nature is;
and this intrinsic imperfection of human affairs
cannot be overcome by procrastination."

Though this is surely far from perfect, I hope it blesses you.

1

LORD, please keep me from listening
   to the advice of the wicked.
Keep me from standing in the path of sinners.
Keep me from sitting in the seat of scoffers.

My delight is in Your law.
Give me the desire and the discipline
   to meditate on it day and night.

I know that, by doing so, I will be like a tree
   firmly planted by streams of water,
   which yields its fruit in its season and
   whose leaf does not wither;
   And in whatever I do, I will prosper.

You tell me that the wicked are not so,
   that they are like chaff which the wind drives away.
You tell me that the wicked will not stand in the judgment,
   nor will sinners be in the assembly of the righteous.
You tell me that You guard the way of the righteous and
   that the way of the wicked will perish.

Please watch over my paths
   and keep me far from the way of the wicked,
   towards which I am so prone to drift.

You guard my way.

1

2

Why are the nations so angry?
Why do they waste their time with futile plans?
The kings of the earth prepare for battle,
    and the rulers plot together against You, LORD,
    and against Your anointed.
"Let us break their chains," they cry,
    "and free ourselves from slavery to God."
But You, the One who sits in the heavens, laugh.
You scoff at them.
You speak to them in Your anger and terrify them
    in Your fury, saying:

    "I HAVE INSTALLED MY KING UPON ZION,
        MY HOLY MOUNTAIN."

I will surely tell of Your decree—that Jesus is Your son
    and that You are His father.
You will give Him the nations as His inheritance
    and the whole earth as His possession.
He will break those who oppose Him with a rod of iron
    and dash them to pieces like pottery.
The rulers of the world, therefore, should act wisely
    and take warning.

I will serve You with reverence and rejoice with trembling.
I will submit to Your Son, that He not become angry,
    and I die in the midst of all my activities,
        for His anger can flare up in an instant.
LORD, what a joy it is to take refuge in Your Son.

> *You are mighty.*
> *You are sovereign.*
> *You are my refuge.*

3

O LORD, I have so many enemies; So many are against me.
So many are saying, "God will never rescue her!"
But You, O LORD, are a shield around me;
    You are my glory and the lifter of my head.

I cry out to You, and You answer from Your holy mountain.
I lay down and slept, and I woke up again, in safety,
    for You were watching over me.
I am not afraid of ten thousand enemies who surround me
    on every side.

Arise, O LORD! Save me, God!
Slap my enemies in the face!
Shatter the teeth of the wicked!
Salvation comes from You, LORD.
Please bless me.

> *You are a shield around me.*
> *You are my glory.*
> *You are the lifter of my head.*
> *You answer me when I cry out to You.*
> *You watch over me.*
> *You save me.*

4

Answer me when I call, O God who declares me innocent!
You have freed me from my troubles;
> Have mercy on me and hear my prayer.

No matter how long people try to ruin my reputation,
> make groundless accusations against me,
> or tell lies about me,

I know that You set apart the godly for Yourself.
You hear me when I call.

I will not sin by letting anger control me.
I will meditate in my heart overnight and remain silent.
I will offer the sacrifices of righteousness and
> trust in You, LORD.

Many people say, "Who will show me better times?"
Let Your face smile on me, LORD.
You have given me greater joy than those
> who have abundant harvests of grain and new wine.

In peace I will lie down and sleep, for You alone, LORD,
> will keep me safe.

You are my liberator.
You hear me when I call.
You give me joy.
You are my protector.

5

O LORD, hear me as I pray;
    Pay attention to my groaning.
Listen to my cry for help, my King and my God,
    for I pray to no one but You.

In the morning, O LORD, You will hear my voice.
In the morning, I will order my prayer to You
    and eagerly watch.
O God, You take no pleasure in wickedness;
    You cannot tolerate the sins of the wicked.

Therefore, the proud will not stand in Your presence,
    for You hate all who do evil.
You will destroy those who tell lies.
You detest murderers and deceivers.

Because of Your unfailing love, I can enter Your house;
    I will worship at Your temple with deepest awe.
Lead me in the right path, O LORD,
    or my enemies will conquer me.
Make Your way plain for me to follow.

My enemies cannot speak a truthful word.
Their deepest desire is to destroy others.
Their talk is foul, like the stench from an open grave.
Their tongues are filled with flattery.

O God, declare them guilty.
Let them be caught in their own traps.
Drive them away because of their many sins,
    for they have rebelled against You.

You take no pleasure in wickedness.

But let all who take refuge in You rejoice;
    Let them sing joyful praises forever.
Spread Your protection over them, that all
    who love Your name may be filled with joy.

For You bless the godly, O LORD;
    You surround them with Your shield of love.

You bless the godly.

6

Lord, don't rebuke me in Your anger
    or discipline me in Your rage.
Have mercy on me, Lord, for I am weak.
Heal me, Lord, for my bones are in agony.
My soul is in deep anguish.
How long, O Lord, until You restore me?

Return, Lord, and rescue me!
Save me because of Your unfailing love.
For the dead do not remember You.
Who can praise You from the grave?

I am exhausted from sobbing;
    All night long I flood my bed with weeping,
    drenching it with my tears.
My vision is blurred by grief;
    My eyes are worn out because of all my enemies.

Lord, make all who behave wickedly depart from me.
For You, O Lord, have heard my weeping.
You have heard my appeal for mercy.
You will answer my prayer.
Make all my enemies be humiliated and terrified.
Make them suddenly turn back in shame.

You answer my prayers.

7

I come to You for protection, O LORD my God.
Save me from my persecutors—rescue me!
If You don't, they will maul me like a lion,
    tearing me to pieces with no one to rescue me.
O LORD my God, if I have done wrong
    or am guilty of injustice,
If I have betrayed a friend
    or plundered my enemy without cause,
        then let my enemies capture me.
Let them trample me into the ground
    and drag my honor in the dust.

Arise, O LORD, in anger!
Stand up against the fury of my enemies!
Wake up, my God, and bring justice!
Gather the nations before You.
Rule over them from on high.
You judge the nations.
Declare me righteous, O LORD,
For I am innocent, O Most High!
End the evil of those who are wicked,
    and defend the righteous.
For You look deep within the mind and heart,
    O righteous God.

God, You are my shield, saving those
    whose hearts are true and right.
You are an honest judge.
You are angry with the wicked every day.

You judge the nations.
You are my shield.

If a person does not repent, You will sharpen Your sword;
    You will bend and string Your bow.
You will prepare Your deadly weapons
    and shoot Your flaming arrows.

The wicked conceive evil;
    They are pregnant with trouble and give birth to lies.
They dig a deep pit to trap others, then fall into it themselves.
The trouble they make for others backfires on them.
The violence they plan falls on their own heads.

I will thank You, LORD, because You are just;
    I will sing praise to Your name, O LORD Most High.

You are just.

8

O Lord, my Lord, how majestic is Your name
in all the earth!
Your glory is higher than the heavens.
You have taught children and infants to tell of Your strength,
silencing Your enemies and all who oppose You.

When I look at the night sky and see the work of Your
fingers—the moon and the stars You set in place—
what are mere mortals that You should think about them,
human beings that You should care for them?
Yet You made them only a little lower than You
and crowned them with glory and honor.
You gave them charge of everything You made,
putting all things under their authority—
the flocks and the herds
and all the wild animals,
the birds in the sky, the fish in the sea,
and everything that swims the ocean currents.

O Lord, my Lord, how majestic is Your name
in all the earth!

You are majestic.
You created everything.

9

I will praise You, LORD, with all my heart;
> I will tell of all the marvelous things You have done.
I will be filled with joy because of You.
I will sing praises to Your name, O Most High.

David's enemies retreated;
> They staggered and died when You appeared.
For You judged in his favor; From Your throne,
> You judged with fairness.
You rebuked the nations and destroyed the wicked;
> You erased their names forever.
The enemy is finished, in endless ruins;
> The cities You uprooted are now forgotten.

But You, LORD, reign forever,
> executing judgment from Your throne.
You will judge the world with justice
> and rule the nations with fairness.
You are a shelter for the oppressed,
> a refuge in times of trouble.
Those who know Your name trust in You.
For You do not abandon those who search for You.

I will sing praises to You who reigns in Jerusalem.
I will tell the world about Your unforgettable deeds.
For You who avenge murder also care for the helpless.
You do not ignore the cries of those who suffer.

You reign forever.
You care for the helpless.
You are a shelter for the oppressed.

LORD, have mercy on me.
See how my enemies torment me.
Snatch me back from the jaws of death.
Save me so I can praise You publicly,
	so I can rejoice that You have rescued me.

The nations have fallen into the pit they dug for others.
Their own feet have been caught in the trap they set.
You are known for Your justice.
The wicked are trapped by their own deeds.

The wicked will go down to the grave.
This is the fate of all the nations who ignore You.
But the needy will not be ignored forever;
	The hopes of the poor will not always be crushed.

Arise, O LORD!
Do not let mere mortals defy You!
Judge the nations! Make them tremble in fear, O LORD.
Let the nations know they are merely human.

You are just.

10

O LORD, why do You stand so far away?
Why do You hide when I am in trouble?
The wicked arrogantly hunt down the poor.
Let them be caught in the evil they plan for others.
For they brag about their evil desires;
> They praise the greedy and curse You.

The wicked are too proud to seek You.
They seem to think that You are dead.
Yet they succeed in everything they do.
They do not see Your punishment awaiting them.
They sneer at all their enemies.
They think, "Nothing bad will ever happen to me!
> We will be free of trouble forever!"

Their mouths are full of cursing, lies, and threats.
Trouble and evil are on the tips of their tongues.
They lurk in ambush in the villages,
> waiting to murder innocent people.
They are always searching for helpless victims.
Like lions crouched in hiding,
> they wait to pounce on the helpless.
Like hunters they capture the helpless
> and drag them away in nets.
Their helpless victims are crushed;
> They fall beneath the strength of the wicked.
The wicked think, "God isn't watching me!
He has closed his eyes and won't even see what I do!"

You are alive.
You see everything.

Arise, O LORD!
Punish the wicked, O God! Do not ignore the helpless!
Why do the wicked get away with despising God?
They think, "God will never call me to account."
But You see the trouble and grief they cause.
You take note of it and punish them.
The helpless put their trust in You.
You defend the orphans.

Break the arms of these wicked, evil people!
Go after them until the last one is humbled
    and brought to you.
You are King forever and ever!

The godless nations will vanish from the land.
LORD, You know the hopes of the helpless.
Surely You will hear their cries and comfort them.
You will bring justice to the orphans and the oppressed,
    so mere people can no longer terrify them.

You defend the orphans and the oppressed.
You are King forever and ever.

11

LORD, I trust You for protection.
The world says to me:

> "Fly like a bird to the mountains for safety!
> The wicked are stringing their bows
>   and fitting their arrows on the bowstrings.
> They shoot from the shadows
>   at those whose hearts are right.
> The foundations of law and order have collapsed.
> What can the righteous do?"

But You, LORD, are in Your holy Temple;
    You still rule from heaven.
You watch everyone closely,
    examining every person on earth.
You examine both the righteous and the wicked.

You hate those who love violence.
You will rain down blazing coals and
    burning sulfur on the wicked,
        punishing them with scorching winds.
You are righteous, LORD, and You love justice.
The virtuous will see Your face.

You rule from heaven.
You are righteous.

12

Help, O LORD, for the godly are fast disappearing!
The faithful have vanished from the earth!

Neighbors lie to each other,
    speaking with flattering lips and deceitful hearts.
LORD, cut off their flattering lips
    and silence their boastful tongues.

They say, "We will lie to our hearts' content.
    Our lips are our own—who can stop us?"

LORD, You reply:

    "I have seen violence done to the helpless,
        and I have heard the groans of the poor.
    Now I will rise up to rescue them,
        as they have longed for Me to do."

LORD, Your promises are pure, like silver
    refined in a furnace, purified seven times over.
Therefore, LORD, I know You will protect the oppressed,
    preserving them forever from this lying generation,
    even though the wicked strut about,
    and evil is praised throughout the land.

Your promises are pure.
You will protect the oppressed.

13

O Lord, how long will You forget me? Forever?
How long will You look the other way?
How long must I struggle with anguish in my soul,
     with sorrow in my heart every day?
How long will my enemy have the upper hand?

Turn and answer me, O Lord my God!
Restore the sparkle to my eyes, or I will die.
Don't let my enemies gloat, saying, "We have defeated her!"
Don't let them rejoice at my downfall.

But I trust in Your unfailing love.
I will rejoice because You have rescued me.
I will sing to You because You are good to me.

You love me.
You saved me.
You are good to me.

14

The fool has said in his heart, "There is no God."
They are corrupt, they have committed abominable deeds;
    There is no one who does good.

Lord, You have looked down from heaven
    on the entire human race;
      To see if there are any who are wise, if any seek after You.
They have all turned aside. They have all become corrupt;
    There is no one who does good, not even one.

Will those who do evil ever learn?
They eat up Your people like bread
    and wouldn't think of praying to You.
But terror will grip them,
    for You are with those who obey You.

Evildoers frustrate the plans of the poor.
But You protect Your people.

Who will come from Mount Zion to rescue Israel?
When You restore Your people, Jacob will shout with joy,
    and Israel will rejoice.

You are with me.
You are my protector.

15

Who may worship in Your sanctuary, LORD?
Who may enter Your presence on Your holy hill?

Those who lead blameless lives and do what is right,
    speaking the truth from sincere hearts.

Those who refuse to gossip
    or harm their neighbors
    or speak evil of their friends.

Those who despise flagrant sinners,
    and honor Your faithful followers,
    and keep their promises even when it hurts.

Those who lend money without charging interest,
    and who cannot be bribed to lie about the innocent.

Such people will stand firm forever.

You are holy.

16

Preserve me, O God, for I take refuge in You.
You are my Lord; I have no good besides You.

The godly people in the land are my true heroes.
I take pleasure in them.

Troubles multiply for those who chase after other gods.
I will not take part in their wickedness
    or even speak the names of their gods.
Nor will I take their names upon my lips.

You alone are my inheritance and my cup of blessing;
    You make my future secure.
The land You have given me is a pleasant land.
What a wonderful inheritance!
I will bless You who guides me;
    Even at night my heart instructs me.

I constantly trust in You;
    You are at my right hand, I will not be shaken.
Therefore my heart is glad, and my whole being rejoices;
    My flesh also dwells securely.

For You will not abandon my soul to Sheol;
    Nor will You allow Your Holy One to undergo decay.
You will make known to me the path of life;
    In Your presence is fullness of joy;
    In Your right hand there are pleasures forever.

> *You are my Lord.*
> *You are my inheritance.*
> *You are my ultimate joy.*

17

O Lord, hear my plea for justice. Listen to my cry for help.
Pay attention to my prayer, for it comes from honest lips.
Declare me innocent, for You see those who do right.

You have tested my thoughts
    and examined my heart in the night.
You have scrutinized me and found nothing wrong.
I am determined not to sin in what I say.
I have followed Your commands,
    which keep me from following cruel and evil people.
My steps have stayed on Your path;
    I have not wavered from following You.

I am praying to You because I know You will answer, O God.
Bend down and listen as I pray.
Show me Your unfailing love in wonderful ways.
By Your mighty power You rescue those
    who seek refuge from their enemies.
Keep me as the apple of Your eye.
Hide me in the shadow of Your wings.

Protect me from wicked people who attack me,
    from murderous enemies who surround me.
They are without pity. Listen to their boasting!
They track me down and surround me,
    watching for the chance to throw me to the ground.
They are like hungry lions,
    eager to tear me apart—like young lions hiding in ambush.

You see those who do right.

Arise, O Lord!
Stand against them, and bring them to their knees!
Rescue me from the wicked with Your sword!
By the power of Your hand, O Lord,
    destroy those who look to this world for their reward.

But satisfy the hunger of Your treasured ones.
Make their children have plenty,
    leaving an inheritance for their descendants.
Because I am righteous, I will see You.
When I awake, I will see You face to face and be satisfied.

You are my protector.

18

I love You, Lord; You are my strength.
You are my rock, my fortress, and my savior;
    You are my God, my rock, in whom I find protection.
You are my shield, the power that saves me,
    and my place of safety.
I called on You, Lord. You are worthy of praise,
    and You saved me from my enemies.

The ropes of death entangled me;
    Floods of destruction swept over me.
The grave wrapped its ropes around me;
    Death laid a trap in my path.
But in my distress I cried out to You, Lord;
    Yes, I prayed to You, my God, for help.
You heard me from Your sanctuary;
    My cry to You reached Your ears.

Then the earth quaked and trembled.
The foundations of the mountains shook;
    They quaked because of Your anger.
Smoke poured from Your nostrils;
    Fierce flames leaped from Your mouth.
Glowing coals blazed forth from You.
You opened the heavens and came down;
    Dark storm clouds were beneath Your feet.

You are my rock.
You are my fortress.
You are my savior.
You are my shield.
You are the power that saves me.
You are my place of safety.
You are worthy of praise.

Mounted on a mighty angelic being, You flew,
    soaring on the wings of the wind.
You shrouded Yourself in darkness,
    veiling Your approach with dark rain clouds.
Thick clouds shielded the brightness around You
    and rained down hail and burning coals.
You thundered from heaven; Your voice, Most High,
    resounded amid the hail and burning coals.
You shot Your arrows and scattered Your enemies;
    Great bolts of lightning flashed, and they were confused.
Then at Your command, O Lord, at the blast of Your breath,
    the bottom of the sea could be seen,
    and the foundations of the earth were laid bare.

You reached down from heaven and rescued me;
    You drew me out of deep waters.
You rescued me from my powerful enemies,
    from those who hated me and were too strong for me.
They attacked me at a moment when I was in distress,
    but You, Lord, supported me.
You led me to a place of safety;
    You rescued me because You delight in me.
You, Lord, rewarded me for doing right;
    You restored me because of my innocence.
For I have kept Your ways, Lord;
    I have not turned from You, my God, to follow evil.
I have followed all Your regulations;
    I have never abandoned Your decrees.
I am blameless before You, God;
    I have kept myself from sin.
You rewarded me for doing right.
You have seen my innocence.

You have rescued me.
You have rewarded me.

To the faithful You show Yourself faithful;
   To those with integrity You show integrity.
To the pure You show Yourself pure,
   but to the crooked You show Yourself shrewd.
You rescue the humble, but You humiliate the proud.
You light a lamp for me.
You light up my darkness O LORD, my God.
In Your strength I can crush an army;
   With You, my God, I can scale any wall.

Your way is perfect. All Your promises prove true.
You are a shield for all who look to You for protection.
For who are You, God, except the LORD?
Who but You, my God, is a solid rock?
You arm me with strength, and You make my way perfect.

You made King David as surefooted as a deer,
   enabling him to stand on mountain heights.
You trained his hands for battle and
   strengthened his arm to draw a bronze bow.
You gave him Your shield of victory.
Your right hand supported him; Your help made him great.
You made a wide path for his feet to keep them from slipping.

He chased his enemies and caught them;
   He did not stop until they were conquered.
He struck them down so they could not get up;
   They fell beneath his feet.
You armed him with strength for the battle;
   You subdued his enemies under his feet.
You placed his foot on their necks.

Your way is perfect.
Your promises prove true.

He destroyed all who hated him.
They called for help, but no one came to their rescue.
They even cried to You, but You refused to answer.
He ground them as fine as dust in the wind.
He swept them into the gutter like dirt.
You gave him victory over his accusers.
You appointed him ruler over nations;
    People he didn't even know began serving him.
As soon as they heard of him, they submitted;
    Foreign nations cringed before him.
They all lost their courage and
    came trembling from their strongholds.

You live, O LORD! Praise be to You, my Rock!
Be exalted, O God of my salvation!
You are the God who pays back those who harm me;
    You subdue the nations under me
    and rescue me from my enemies.
You hold me safe beyond the reach of my enemies;
    You save me from violent opponents.

For this, O LORD, I will praise You among the nations;
    I will sing praises to Your name.
You gave great victories to David, Your king;
    You showed unfailing love to Your anointed,
    to David and all his descendants forever.

O LORD, show Your unfailing love to me.

You live.
Your love is unfailing.

19

The heavens proclaim Your glory, God.
The skies display Your craftsmanship.
Day after day they continue to speak;
    Night after night they make You known.
They speak without a sound or word;
    Their voice is never heard.
Yet their message has gone throughout the earth,
    and their words to all the world.

You have made a home in the heavens for the sun.
It bursts forth like a radiant bridegroom after his wedding.
It rejoices like a great athlete eager to run the race.
The sun also rises at one end of the heavens
    and follows its course to the other end.
Nothing can hide from its heat.

Your law is perfect, LORD, restoring the soul;
    Your testimony is sure, making wise the simple.
Your precepts are right, rejoicing the heart;
    Your commandment is pure, enlightening the eyes.

You are the mighty Creator.
Your law is perfect.
Your testimony is sure.
Your precepts are right.
Your commandment is pure.

Reverence for You is pure, lasting forever;
    Your laws are true; Each one is fair.
They are more desirable than gold, even the finest gold;
    They are sweeter than honey,
    even honey dripping from the comb.
They are a warning to Your servant,
    a great reward for those who obey them.

How can I know all the sins lurking in my heart?
Acquit me of these hidden faults.
Keep Your servant from deliberate sins.
Don't let them control me.
Then I will be blameless and innocent of great sin.
Let the words of my mouth
    and the meditation of my heart
    be acceptable in Your sight,
    O LORD, my Rock and my Redeemer.

Your laws are true.
Your laws are sweeter than honey.
Your laws are a warning.
Your laws are a reward.
You are my rock.
You are my redeemer.

20

In times of trouble, LORD, answer my cry.
O God of Jacob, keep me safe from all harm.
Send me help and strengthen me.
Remember me and look favorably upon me.

Grant my heart's desires and make all my plans succeed.
I will shout for joy when I am victorious and
    raise a victory banner in Your name.
LORD, answer all my prayers.

Now I know that You rescued Your anointed king, David.
You answered him from Your holy heaven
    and rescued him by Your great power.

Some boast in chariots and some in horses,
    but I will boast in Your name, O LORD, my God.
Those nations will fall down and collapse,
    but I will rise up and stand firm.

Give me victory, O LORD!
Answer my cry for help.

> *You answer my prayers.*
> *Your name alone is powerful.*

21

I rejoice in Your strength, O Lord!
I shout with joy because You give me victory
For You have given me my heart's desire.
You have withheld nothing I requested.

You welcomed me back with success and prosperity.
You placed a crown of finest gold on my head.
I asked You to preserve my life,
    and You granted my request.
The days of my life stretch on forever.
Your victory brings me great honor,
    and You have clothed me with splendor and majesty.
You have endowed me with eternal blessings
    and given me the joy of Your presence.
I trust in You, Lord.
Your unfailing love will keep me from stumbling.

You will capture all Your enemies.
Your strong right hand will seize all who hate You.
You will throw them in a flaming furnace when You appear.
You will consume them in Your anger.
Fire will devour them.
You will wipe their children from the face of the earth.
They will never have descendants.
Although they plot against You,
    their evil schemes will never succeed.
For they will turn and run
    when they see Your arrows aimed at them.

Rise up, O Lord, in all Your power.
With music and singing I celebrate Your mighty acts.

You are all powerful.

22

My God, my God, why have You abandoned me?
Why are You so far away when I groan for help?
Every day I call to You, my God, but You do not answer.
Every night I lift my voice, but I find no relief.

Yet You are holy, enthroned on the praises of Israel.
My ancestors trusted in You, and You rescued them.
They cried out to You and were saved.
They trusted in You and were never disgraced.

But I am a worm and not a woman.
I am scorned and despised by all!
Everyone who sees me mocks me.
They sneer and shake their heads, saying:

> "Is this the one who relies on the LORD?
> Then let the LORD save her!
> If the LORD loves her so much, let the LORD rescue her!"

Yet You brought me safely from my mother's womb
    and led me to trust You at my mother's breast.
I was thrust into Your arms at my birth.
You have been my God from the moment I was born.

Do not stay so far from me, for trouble is near,
    and no one else can help me.
Your Son's enemies surrounded Him like a herd of bulls;
    Fierce bulls of Bashan hemmed Him in!

You are holy.

Like lions they open their jaws against Him,
    roaring and tearing into their prey.
His life was poured out like water,
    and all His bones were out of joint.
His heart was like wax, melting within Him.
His strength dried up like sunbaked clay.
His tongue stuck to the roof of His mouth.
You laid Him in the dust and left Him for dead.
His enemies surrounded Him like a pack of dogs;
    An evil gang closed in on Him.
They pierced His hands and feet.
Though all His bones could be counted,
    His enemies stared at Him and gloated.
They divided His garments among themselves
    and threw dice for His clothing.

O Lord, do not stay far away!
You are my strength; Come quickly to my aid!
Save me from the sword;
    Spare my precious life from these dogs.
Snatch me from the lion's jaws
    and from the horns of these wild oxen.

I will proclaim Your name to my brothers and sisters.
I will praise You among Your assembled people.
I praise You, Lord, as one who fears You.
I honor You. I show You reverence.
For You have not ignored or belittled
    the suffering of the needy.
You have not turned Your back on them,
    but have listened to their cries for help.

You are holy.
You listen to the cries of the needy.

I will praise You in the great assembly.
I will fulfill my vows in the presence
    of those who worship You.
The poor will eat and be satisfied.

All who seek You, Lord, will praise You.
Their hearts will rejoice with everlasting joy.
The whole earth will acknowledge You, Lord,
    and return to You.
All the families of the nations will bow down before You.
For royal power belongs to You, Lord.
You rule all the nations.

Let the rich of the earth feast and worship.
I will bow before You, as one who is mortal,
    whose life will end as dust.
My children will also serve You.
Future generations will hear about Your wonders, Lord.
Your righteous acts will be told to those not yet born.
They will hear about everything You have done.

You rule all the nations.

23

You are my shepherd. I shall not want.

You make me lie down in green pastures;
    You lead me beside quiet waters.

You restore my soul;
    You guide me in the paths of righteousness
    for Your name's sake.

Even though I walk through the valley
    of the shadow of death,
    I fear no evil, for You are with me;
    Your rod and Your staff, they comfort me.

You prepare a table before me in the presence of my enemies;
    You have anointed my head with oil; My cup overflows.

Surely goodness and lovingkindness
    will follow me all the days of my life,
    and I will dwell in Your house forever.

You are my shepherd.
You are with me.
You are my inheritance.

24

The earth is Yours and all it contains.
The world and those who dwell in it belong to You.
For You founded it upon the seas and
    established it upon the ocean currents.

Who may climb Your mountain, Lord?
And who may stand in Your holy dwelling place?
Only those whose hands and hearts are pure,
    who do not worship idols and never tell lies.
They will receive Your blessing
    and have a right relationship with You, Lord, my Savior.
Such people may seek You and worship in Your presence,
    O God of Jacob.

Lord, let the ancient gates be opened
    let the ancient doors be lifted,
      that You, the King of glory, may come in!
Who is the King of glory?
You are the Lord, strong and mighty.
You are invincible in battle.

Lord, let the ancient gates be opened;
    Let the ancient doors be lifted,
      that You, the King of glory, may come in!
Who is this King of glory?
You are the Lord of Heaven's Armies.
You are the King of glory.

You are invincible in battle.
You are the King of Glory.

25

O LORD, I give my life to You.
I trust in You, my God!
Do not let me be disgraced,
    or let my enemies rejoice in my defeat.
No one who trusts in You will ever be disgraced,
    but disgrace comes to those who try to deceive others.

Show me the right path, O LORD;
    Point out the road for me to follow.
Lead me by Your truth and teach me,
    for You are the God who saves me.
All day long I put my hope in You.
Remember, O LORD, Your compassion and unfailing love,
    for You have always acted in this manner.
Do not remember the rebellious sins of my youth.
Remember me in the light of Your unfailing love,
    for You are merciful, O LORD.

LORD, You are good, and You do what is right.
You teach sinners the right way to live.
You lead the humble in doing right, teaching them Your way.
You always prove faithful and reliable
    to those who follow the demands of Your covenant.
For Your name's sake, O LORD,
    pardon my iniquity, for it is great.

Who are those who fear You, LORD?
You will show me the path I should choose.
I will live in prosperity, and my children will inherit the land.

You are merciful.
You are good.
You do what is right.

You, LORD, are a friend to me.
You teach me Your covenant.
My eyes are always on You, LORD,
    for You rescue me from the traps of my enemies.

Turn to me and be gracious to me,
    for I am lonely and afflicted.
My problems go from bad to worse.
Oh, save me from them all!

Feel my pain, and see my trouble.
Forgive all my sins.
See how many enemies I have
    and how viciously they hate me!
Protect me!
Rescue my life from them!

Do not let me be disgraced, for in You I take refuge.
May integrity and honesty protect me,
    for I put my hope in You.
O God, ransom me from all my troubles.

You are my friend.
You rescue me.
You are my hope.

26

Vindicate me, O LORD, for I have integrity,
  and I trust in You, LORD, without wavering.
Examine me, O LORD, and test me!
Evaluate my inner thoughts and motives!
For I am ever aware of Your faithfulness,
  and Your loyalty continually motivates me.

I do not associate with deceitful men
  or consort with those who are dishonest.
I hate the mob of evil men
  and do not associate with the wicked.
I maintain a pure lifestyle,
  so I can appear before Your altar, O LORD,
  to give You thanks and to tell about
  all Your amazing deeds.
I love Your sanctuary, LORD,
  the place where Your glorious presence dwells.

Don't let me suffer the fate of sinners.
Don't condemn me along with murderers.
Their hands are dirty with evil schemes,
  and they constantly take bribes.

But I am not like that; I live with integrity.
Rescue me and have mercy on me!

I am safe; And I will publicly praise You, LORD.

You are faithful.

27

Lord, You are my light and my salvation,
    so why should I be afraid?
You are my fortress, protecting me from danger,
    so why should I tremble?
When evil men attack me,
    when my enemies and foes attack me,
    they stumble and fall.
Though a mighty army surrounds me,
    my heart will not be afraid.
Even if I am attacked, I will remain confident.

The one thing I ask of You, Lord—the thing I seek most—
    is to live in Your house all the days of my life,
    delighting in Your perfections
    and meditating in Your temple.

For You will conceal me there when troubles come;
    You will hide me in Your sanctuary.
You will place me out of reach on a high rock.
Then I will hold my head high above my enemies
    who surround me.
I will offer sacrifices in Your dwelling place
    and shout for joy!
I will sing praises to You.

Hear me as I pray, O Lord. Be merciful and answer me!
My heart has heard You say, "Come and talk with me."
And my heart responds, "Lord, I am coming."

You are my light.
You are my salvation.
You are my fortress.

Do not turn Your back on me.
Do not reject Your servant in anger.
You have always been my helper.
Don't leave me now;
    Don't abandon me, O God of my salvation!
Even if my father and mother abandon me,
    You will hold me close.

Teach me how to live, O LORD.
Lead me along the right path,
    for my enemies are waiting for me.
Do not let me fall into their hands.
For they accuse me of things I've never done;
    With every breath, they threaten me with violence.
Yet I am confident I will see Your goodness
    while I am here in the land of the living.

I wait patiently for You, LORD.
I will be brave and courageous, as I wait patiently for You.

You will never abandon me.

28

I pray to You, O Lord, my Rock.
Do not turn a deaf ear to me.
For if You are silent, I might as well give up and die.
Listen to my prayer for mercy, as I cry out to You for help,
    as I lift my hands toward Your holy sanctuary.
Do not drag me away with evil men,
    with those who behave wickedly,
    who speak friendly words to their neighbors
    while planning evil in their hearts.
Give them the punishment they so richly deserve!
Measure it out in proportion to their wickedness.
Pay them back for all their evil deeds!
Give them a taste of what they have done to others.
For they do not understand Your actions or
    the way You carry out justice.
You will permanently demolish them.

I praise You, Lord! For You have heard my cry for mercy.
You are my strength and shield. I trust You with all my heart.
You help me, and my heart is filled with joy.
I burst out in songs of thanksgiving.
You give Your people strength.
You are a safe fortress for Your anointed king.
Save Your people!
Bless Israel, Your special possession.
Lead them like a shepherd,
    and carry them in Your arms forever.

You are just.
You hear me.
You are my strength.
You help me.
You fill my heart with joy.

29

I honor You, LORD.
I honor You for Your majesty and power.
I honor You for the glory of Your name.
I worship You, LORD, in the splendor of Your holiness.
Your shout echoes above the sea.
You, the God of glory, thunder over the mighty sea.

Your shout is powerful.
Your shout is majestic.
Your shout breaks the cedars.
You shatter the cedars of Lebanon.
You make Lebanon skip like a calf
    and Sirion like a young ox.
Your shout strikes with flaming fire.
Your shout shakes the wilderness.
You shake the wilderness of Kadesh.
Your shout bends the large trees
    and strips the leaves from the forests.

Everyone in Your temple says, "Majestic!"
You sit enthroned over the engulfing waters.
You sit enthroned as the eternal king.
You give Your people strength;
    You grant Your people security.

You are majestic.
You are the Eternal King.

30

I will praise You, Lord, for You rescued me.
You refused to let my enemies triumph over me.
O Lord my God, I cried to You for help, and You healed me.
You brought me up from the grave, O Lord.
You kept me from falling into the pit of death.

I will sing praise to You, Lord.
I will praise Your holy name.
For Your anger lasts only a moment,
    but Your favor lasts a lifetime!
Weeping may last through the night,
    but a shout of joy comes in the morning.

When I was prosperous, I said, "Nothing can stop me now!"
Your favor, O Lord, made me as secure as a mountain.
Then You turned away from me, and I was shattered.
I cried out to You, O Lord.
I begged You for mercy, saying:

    "What will You gain if I die, if I sink into the grave?
    Can the dust praise You?
    Can it tell of Your faithfulness?
    Hear me, Lord, and have mercy on me.
    Help me, O Lord."

You have turned my mourning into joyful dancing.
You have taken away my clothes of mourning
    and clothed me with joy,
        that I might sing praises to You and not be silent.

O Lord my God, I will give thanks to You forever!

You heal me.
You turn my sorrow to joy.

31

In You, Lord, I have taken refuge.
Let me never be put to shame.
Deliver me in Your righteousness.
Turn Your ear to me. Come quickly to my rescue.
Be my rock of refuge, a strong fortress to save me.
Since You are my rock and my fortress,
 for the sake of Your name, lead and guide me.
Keep me free from the trap that is set for me,
 for You are my refuge.
Into Your hands I commit my spirit.
Deliver me, Lord, my faithful God.

I hate those who cling to worthless idols;
 As for me, I trust in You, Lord.
I will be glad and rejoice in Your love,
 for You saw my affliction and
 knew the anguish of my soul.
You have not given me into the hands of the enemy
 but have set my feet in a spacious place.

Have mercy on me, Lord, for I am in distress.
Tears blur my eyes.
My body and soul are withering away.
I am dying from grief; My years are shortened by sadness.
Sin has drained my strength; I am wasting away from within.

I feel like David—scorned by my enemies,
 despised by my neighbors, and avoided by my friends.
I feel like when they see me on the street,
 they go the other way.
I feel ignored as if I were dead, as if I were a broken pot.

You are my refuge.

I have heard many rumors about me,
    and I am surrounded by terror.
I feel like I have enemies conspiring against me,
    plotting to take my life.
But I am trusting You, O Lord, saying, "You are my God!"
My future is in Your hands.
Rescue me from those who hunt me down relentlessly.
Let Your favor shine on Your servant.
In Your unfailing love, rescue me.
Don't let me be disgraced, O Lord,
    for I call out to You for help.
Let the wicked be disgraced; Let them lie silent in the grave.
Silence their lying lips—those proud and arrogant lips
    that accuse the godly.

How great is the goodness You have stored up
    for those who fear You.
You lavish it on those who come to You for protection,
    blessing them before the watching world.
You hide them in the shelter of Your presence,
    safe from those who conspire against them.
You shelter them in Your presence,
    far from accusing tongues.

Praise be to You, Lord, for You have
    shown me the wonders of Your unfailing love.
You kept me safe when I was under attack.
In my alarm I said, "I am cut off from Your sight!"
Yet You heard my cry for mercy
    when I called to You for help.
I love You, Lord, along with all Your faithful people!
You preserve those who are true to You,
    but the proud You pay back in full.
I will be strong and take heart, for my hope is in You, Lord.

You are my hope.

45

32

Oh, what joy for those whose disobedience is forgiven,
    whose sin is put out of sight!
Yes, what joy for those whose record You have cleared
    of guilt, whose lives are lived in complete honesty!
When I refused to confess my sin, my body wasted away,
    and I groaned all day long.
Day and night Your hand of discipline was heavy on me.
My strength evaporated like water in the summer heat.

Finally, I confessed all my sins to You
    and stopped trying to hide my guilt.
I said to myself, "I will confess my rebellion to the LORD."
And You forgave me! All my guilt is gone.

Therefore, let all the godly pray to You
    while there is still time, that they may not drown
    in the floodwaters of judgment.
For You are my hiding place.
You protect me from trouble.
You surround me with songs of deliverance.

LORD, thank You for guiding me
    and teaching me in the way I should go
    and for advising me and watching over me.
I will listen to Your counsel so that I will not be
    like a senseless horse or mule that has no understanding
    and needs a bit and bridle to keep it under control.
Many sorrows come to the wicked,
    but unfailing love surrounds those who trust You, LORD.
So I rejoice in You, LORD, and are glad, as I obey You.
I will shout for joy, for You have made my heart pure!

You are my hiding place.
You are my guide.

33

I will sing for joy to You, LORD.
It is fitting for me to praise You.
I will praise You with music.
I will sing a new song of praise to You and sing with joy.
For Your word holds true, and I can trust everything You do.
You love whatever is just and good.
Your unfailing love fills the earth.

You merely spoke, and the heavens were created.
You breathed the word, and all the stars were born.
You assigned the sea its boundaries
    and locked the oceans in vast reservoirs.
Let the whole world fear You, LORD,
    and let everyone stand in awe of You.
For when You spoke, the world began!
It appeared at Your command.
You frustrate the plans of the nations
    and thwart all their schemes.
But Your plans stand firm forever.
Your intentions can never be shaken.
What joy for the nation whose God is You, LORD,
    whose people You have chosen as Your inheritance.

You watch from heaven and see the whole human race.
From Your throne You observe all who live on the earth.
You made their hearts, so You understand everything they do.
The best-equipped army cannot save a king,
    nor is great strength enough to save a warrior.
I cannot count on my greatest strengths
    or allies to give me victory.
All my skills, shrewdness, and strength cannot save me.

You are Creator of all.

But You watch over those who fear You,
    those who rely on Your unfailing love.
You rescue them from death
    and keep them alive in times of famine.
I put my hope in You, LORD.
You are my help and my shield.
In You my heart rejoices, for I trust in Your holy name.
Let Your unfailing love surround me, LORD,
    for my hope is in You alone.

You are my hope.
You are my help.
You are my shield.

34

I will praise You, LORD, at all times.
I will constantly speak Your praises.
I will boast only in You, LORD.
Let all who are helpless take heart.
I will tell of Your greatness
    and exalt Your name with those around me.

I pray to You, and You answer me.
You free me from all my fears.
Those who look to You for help will be radiant with joy,
    and their faces will never be ashamed.
In my desperation I prayed,
    and You listened and saved me from all my troubles.
For Your angel is a guard, who surrounds
    and defends all who fear You.

LORD, help me to taste and see that You are good.
Oh, the joys of those who take refuge in You.
LORD, teach me to fear You, for I know that all those
    who fear You will have all they need.
Even strong young lions sometimes go hungry,
    but those who trust in You will lack no good thing.
I will listen to You, LORD, teach me to fear You.
I want to live a life that is long and prosperous.
Help me keep my tongue from speaking evil
    and my lips from telling lies.
Help me turn away from evil and do good.
Give me a heart that longs to search for peace
    and that works to maintain it.

> *You are great.*
> *You answer me.*
> *You free me from all my fears.*

Your eyes watch over those who do right.
Your ears are open to their cries for help.
But You turn Your face against those who do evil
and will erase their memory from the earth.
You hear Your people when they call to You for help.
You rescue them from all their troubles.
You are near to the brokenhearted
and save those who are crushed in spirit.

The righteous person faces many troubles,
but You come to the rescue each time.
You protect all his bones and not one of them is broken.
Calamity will surely destroy the wicked,
and those who hate the righteous will be punished.
But You, Lord, will redeem those who serve You.
No one who takes refuge in You will be condemned.

You rescue me from all my troubles.
You are near to me when I am brokenhearted.

35

O LORD, I confess that at times I want You
    to oppose those who oppose me
    and fight those who fight against me,
    to put on Your armor and take up Your shield,
    to prepare for battle and come to my aid,
    to lift up Your spear and javelin
    against those who pursue me.

I confess that I want to hear You say,
    "I will give You victory!"
    and, at times, I want You to bring shame and disgrace
    on those trying to kill me,
    to turn them back and
    humiliate those who want to harm me.

I confess that at times I want You
    to blow them away like chaff in the wind—
    a wind sent by Your angel,
    to make their path dark and slippery,
    with Your angel pursuing them.
I did them no wrong, but they laid a trap for me.
I did them no wrong, but they dug a pit to catch me.
This makes me want to ask You
    to let sudden ruin come upon them,
    to let them be caught in the trap they set for me, and
    to let them be destroyed in the pit they dug for me.

But, LORD, You tell me to pray for my enemies
    and that vengeance is Yours.
So, I rejoice in You, LORD.
I am glad because You rescue me.

You rescue me.

With every bone in my body I praise You:

> "LORD, who can compare with You?
> Who else rescues the helpless from the strong?
> Who else protects the helpless and poor
>> from those who rob them?"

Malicious witnesses testify against me.
They accuse me of crimes I know nothing about.
They repay me evil for good. I am sick with despair.
Yet when they were ill, I grieved for them.
I denied myself by fasting for them,
> but my prayers returned unanswered.
I was sad, as though they were my friends or family,
> as if I were grieving for my own mother.
But they are glad now that I am in trouble;
> They gleefully join together against me.
I am attacked by people I don't even know;
> They slander me constantly.
They mock me and call me names;
> They snarl at me.

How long, O Lord, will You look on and do nothing?
Rescue me from their fierce attacks.
Protect my life from these lions!
Then I will thank You in front of the great assembly.
I will praise You before all the people.
Don't let my treacherous enemies rejoice over my defeat.
Don't let those who hate me without cause
> gloat over my sorrow.
They don't talk of peace;
> They plot against innocent people
> who mind their own business.
They shout, "Aha! Aha! With my own eyes I saw her do it!"

You vindicate me.

O LORD, You know all about this.
Do not stay silent. Do not abandon me now, O Lord.
Wake up! Rise to my defense!
Take up my case, my God and my Lord.

Declare me not guilty, O LORD my God, for You give justice.
Don't let my enemies laugh about me in my troubles.
Don't let them say:

"Look, I got what I wanted! Now I will eat her alive!"

Make those who rejoice at my troubles
    be humiliated and disgraced.
Make those who triumph over me
    be covered with shame and dishonor.
But give great joy to those who come to my defense.
Let them continually say:

"Great is the LORD, who delights
    in blessing His servant with peace!"

Then I will proclaim Your justice,
    and I will praise You all day long.

You are just.

36

Sin whispers to the wicked, deep within their hearts.
They have no fear of You at all.
In their blind conceit,
    they cannot see how wicked they really are.
Everything they say is crooked and deceitful.
They refuse to act wisely or do good.
They lie awake at night, hatching sinful plots.
Their actions are never good.
They make no attempt to turn from evil.

Your unfailing love, O Lord, is as vast as the heavens.
Your faithfulness reaches beyond the clouds.
Your righteousness is like the mighty mountains.
Your justice like the ocean depths.
You care for people and animals alike, O Lord.
How precious is Your unfailing love, O God!
All humanity finds shelter in the shadow of Your wings.
You feed them from the abundance of Your own house,
    letting them drink from Your river of delights.
For You are the fountain of life, the light by which I see.

Pour out Your unfailing love on those who love You;
    Give justice to those with honest hearts.
Don't let the proud trample me
    or the wicked push me around.
Look! Those who do evil have fallen!
They are thrown down, never to rise again.

You are the fountain of life.
Your love never fails.

37

LORD, help me to not worry about the wicked
    or envy those who do wrong.
For I know that, like grass, they soon fade away,
    and like spring flowers, they soon wither.
Help me to trust in You, to do good,
    to dwell in the land, and to cultivate faithfulness.
Help me to delight myself in You. For, I know that,
    when I do, You give me the desires of my heart.
LORD, I commit my way to You. I put my trust in You,
    for I know that, when I do, You will help me.
You will make my innocence radiate like the dawn,
    and the justice of my cause will shine like the noonday sun.

Teach me to rest in Your presence,
    and to wait patiently for You to act.
Give me the confidence to not worry about evil people
    who prosper or fret about their wicked schemes.
Please take away my anger and help me to turn from my rage.
For I know that, when I lose my temper, it only leads to harm.

You assure me that the wicked will be destroyed,
    but those who trust in You will possess the land.
Soon the wicked will disappear.
Though I may look for them, they will be gone.
The humble will possess the land
    and will live in peace and prosperity.

> *You give me the desires of my heart.*
> *You will destroy the wicked.*

Though the wicked plot against the godly
    and snarl at them in defiance, You just laugh,
    for You see their day of judgment coming.

Though the wicked draw their swords and string their bows
    to kill the poor and the oppressed,
    to slaughter those who do right,
    their swords will stab their own hearts,
    and their bows will be broken.

I know that it is better to be godly and have little
    than to be evil and rich.
For the strength of the wicked will be shattered,
    but You take care of the godly.
Day by day, You take care of the innocent,
    and I will receive an inheritance that lasts forever.

I will not be disgraced in hard times;
    Even in famine I know I will have more than enough.
But the wicked will die.
LORD, Your enemies are like flowers in a field—
    they will vanish like smoke.

The wicked borrow and never repay,
    but the godly are generous givers.
Those You bless, LORD, will possess the land,
    but those You curse will surely die.

You take care of the godly.
You take care of the innocent.

You direct the steps of the godly.
You delight in every detail of my life.
Though I stumble, I will never fall,
    for You hold me by the hand.
Once I was young, and now I am old.
Yet I have never seen the godly abandoned
    or my children begging for bread.
Give me the faith and courage
    to give generous loans to others.
I know my children are a blessing.

Give me the wisdom and courage to turn from evil
    and do good, that I may live in the land forever.
For You love justice, and You will never abandon the godly.
You will keep me safe forever,
    but the children of the wicked will die.

The godly will possess the land and will live there forever.
Give me Your words that I may offer good counsel
    and teach right from wrong.
Implant Your law in my heart, LORD,
    that I may never slip from my path.
The wicked wait in ambush for the godly,
    looking for an excuse to kill me.

You direct the steps of the godly.
You delight in every detail of my life.
You hold me by the hand.
You love justice.
You will never abandon me.
You will keep me safe forever.

But You will not let the wicked succeed
	or let the godly be condemned when I am put on trial.
I put my hope in You, LORD, and strive to keep Your way.
You will honor me by giving me the land
	and allowing me to see the wicked destroyed.

I have seen wicked and ruthless people
	flourishing like a tree in its native soil.
But when I looked again, they were gone!
Though I searched for them, I could not find them!
I look at those who are honest and good.

I know that a wonderful future awaits those who love peace.
But the rebellious will be destroyed and have no future.
You rescue the godly,
	and You are my fortress in times of trouble.
You help me, rescuing me from the wicked.
You save me, and I find shelter in You.

You will not let the wicked succeed.
You will not let me be condemned.
You will honor me.
You will destroy the rebellious.
You will rescue me.
You are my fortress.
You help me.
You rescue me from the wicked.
You save me.
You are my shelter.

38

O LORD, don't rebuke me in Your anger
    or discipline me in Your rage!
Your arrows have struck deep,
    and Your blows are crushing me.
Because of Your anger, my whole body is sick;
    My health is broken because of my sins.
My guilt overwhelms me—it is a burden too heavy to bear.
My wounds fester and stink because of my foolish sins.
I am bent over and racked with pain.
All day long I walk around filled with grief.
A raging fever burns within me, and my health is broken.
I am exhausted and completely crushed.
My groans come from an anguished heart.

You know what I long for, Lord; You hear my every sigh.
My heart beats wildly, my strength fails,
    and I am going blind.
My loved ones and friends stay away, fearing my disease.
Even my own family stands at a distance.
Meanwhile, my enemies lay traps to kill me.
Those who wish me harm make plans to ruin me.
All day long they plan their treachery.

But I am deaf to all their threats.
I am silent before them as one who cannot speak.
I choose to hear nothing, and I make no reply.
For I am waiting for You, O LORD.
You must answer for me, O Lord my God.
I prayed, "Don't let my enemies gloat over me
    or rejoice at my downfall."

You hear my every sigh.

I am on the verge of collapse, facing constant pain.
But I confess my sins;
    I am deeply sorry for what I have done.
I have many aggressive enemies;
    They hate me without reason.
They repay me evil for good
    and oppose me for pursuing good.

Do not abandon me, O Lord.
Do not stand at a distance, my God.
Come quickly to help me, O Lord my savior.

You are my Savior.

39

I said to myself,
    "I will watch what I do and not sin in what I say.
    I will hold my tongue when the ungodly are around me."

But as I stood there in silence—not even speaking
    of good things—the turmoil within me grew worse.
The more I thought about it, the hotter I got,
    igniting a fire of words:

    "LORD, remind me how brief my time on earth will be.
    Remind me that my days are numbered—
        how fleeting my life is.
    You have made my life no longer
        than the width of my hand.
    My entire lifetime is just a moment to You;
        At best, I am but a breath."

I am merely a moving shadow,
    and all my busy rushing ends in nothing.
I amass riches, not knowing who will spend it.
And so, LORD, where do I put my hope?
My only hope is in You.

You are my only hope.

Rescue me from my rebellion.
Do not let fools mock me.
I am silent before You;
    I won't say a word, for my punishment is from You.
But please stop striking me!
I am exhausted by the blows from Your hand.

When You discipline me for my sins,
    You consume like a moth what is precious to me.
I am but a breath.

Hear my prayer, O Lord!
Listen to my cries for help!
Don't ignore my tears.

For I am Your guest—a traveler passing through,
    as my ancestors were before me.
Leave me alone so I can smile again
    before I am gone and exist no more.

You discipline me.

40

I waited patiently for You, LORD,
    and You turned to me and heard my cry.
You lifted me out of the pit of despair, out of the miry clay.
You set my feet upon a rock making my footsteps firm.
You have given me a new song to sing,
    a song of praise to You, my God.
Many will see and fear and will trust in You.

Oh, the joys of those who trust You, LORD,
    who have no confidence in the proud
    or in those who worship idols.
O LORD my God, You have performed many wonders for me.
Your plans for me are too numerous to list.
You have no equal.
If I tried to recite all Your wonderful deeds,
    I would never come to the end of them.

You take no delight in sacrifices or offerings.
Now that You have made me listen, I finally understand—
    You don't require burnt offerings or sin offerings.

Here I am, I have come.
I take joy in doing Your will, my God,
    for Your instructions are written on my heart.

You turn to me.
You hear my cries.
You lift me out of despair.
You give me a new song to sing.
You have no equal.
You take no delight in sacrifices.

I have told all Your people about Your justice.
I have not been afraid to speak out,
  as You, O Lord, well know.
I have not kept the good news
  of Your justice hidden in my heart;
  I have talked about Your faithfulness and saving power.
I have told everyone in the great assembly
  of Your unfailing love and faithfulness.
Lord, don't hold back Your tender mercies from me.
Let Your unfailing love and faithfulness always protect me.
For troubles surround me—too many to count!
My sins pile up so high I can't see my way out.
They outnumber the hairs on my head.
I have lost all courage.

Please, Lord, rescue me!
Come quickly, Lord, and help me.
Make those who try to destroy me
  be humiliated and put to shame.
Make those who take delight in my trouble
  be turned back in disgrace.
Let them be horrified by their shame, for they said,
  "Aha! We've got her now!"
But may all who search for You
  be filled with joy and gladness in You.
May those who love Your salvation
  repeatedly shout, "The Lord is great!"
As for me, since I am poor and needy,
  Lord keep me in Your thoughts.
You are my helper and my savior.
O my God, do not delay.

You are faithful.
Your love is unfailing.
You are great!
You are my helper and my savior.

41

How blessed are those who treat the poor properly!
When trouble comes, LORD, You will deliver them.
Protect them and keep them alive.
Give them prosperity in the land,
    and rescue them from their enemies.
LORD, nurse them when they are sick
    and restore them to health.

O LORD, have mercy on me!
Heal me, for I have sinned against You!

I feel like David, when his enemies said nothing
    but cruel things about him,
    "When will he finally die and be forgotten?" they asked.
They came to visit and pretended to be his friends,
    but all the while they were thinking of ways to defame him,
    and when they left they would slander him.
All who hated him whispered insults
    about him to one another; and planned ways to harm him.
They said, "He has some fatal disease,
    and he will never get out of that bed."
Even his best friend, whom he trusted completely,
    one who shared meals with him, turned against him.

You care for the poor.
You are the Great Healer.

O LORD, have mercy on me and raise me up,
    so I can repay my enemies with love!
I know You are pleased with me,
    for my enemies do not triumph over me.
You have preserved my life because I am innocent;
    You allow me permanent access to Your presence.

I praise You, LORD, O God of Israel,
In the future and forevermore!
Amen and Amen.

You give me access to Your presence.
You are worthy of all praise.

42

As the deer pants for the water brooks,
   so my soul pants for You, O God.
My soul thirsts for You—the living God;
   When shall I come and appear before You, God?
My tears have been my food day and night,
   while my enemies continually taunt me,
   saying, "Where is Your God?"

My heart is breaking as I remember how it used to be.
For I used to walk among the crowds of worshipers,
   leading a great procession to the house of God,
   singing for joy and giving thanks
   amid the sound of a great celebration.

Why am I discouraged?
Why is my heart so sad?
I will put my hope in You.
I will praise You again—my Savior and my God.

O my God, my soul is in despair within me.
Therefore I will remember You—even from distant places.
One deep stream calls out to another
   at the sound of Your waterfalls;
   All Your breakers and Your waves have rolled over me.

But each day, LORD, You pour Your unfailing love upon me,
   and through each night I sing Your songs,
   praying to You who gives me life.

You are alive.
You are the Living Water.
You are my savior.
You are my God.
You give me life.

O God, my rock, why have You forgotten me?
Why do I wander around in grief, oppressed by my enemies?
Their taunts break my bones.
They scoff, "Where is Your God?"

Why am I discouraged?
Why is my heart so sad?
I will put my hope in You.
I will praise You again—my Savior and my God.

> *You are my rock.*
> *You have not forgotten me.*
> *You are my Savior.*
> *You are my God.*

43

Declare me innocent, O God!
Defend me against these ungodly people.
Rescue me from these unjust liars.

For You are God, my only safe haven.
Why have You tossed me aside?
Why must I wander around in grief,
    oppressed by my enemies?

Send out Your light and Your truth; Let them guide me.
Let them lead me to Your holy mountain,
    to the place where You live.

There I will go to Your altar,
    to You—the source of all my joy.
I will praise You, O God, my God!

Why am I discouraged?
Why is my heart so sad?
I will put my hope in You!
I will praise You again—my Savior and my God!

You are my only safe haven.
You are the source of all my joy.
You are my Savior.
You are my God.

44

O God, remind me what all You did in ancient times.
You drove out the pagan nations by Your power
    and gave all the land to Your people.
You crushed the people living there
    and enabled Your people to occupy it.
Your people did not conquer the land by their swords,
    and they did not prevail by their strength.
But it was Your right hand and strong arm
    and the blinding light from Your face that helped them,
    for You favored them.

You are my King and my God.
As You commanded victories for Israel,
    empowering it to push back its enemies
    and, in Your name, trample its foes,
    I will not put my trust in my abilities
    nor count on my strength to save me.
You are the one who gives me victory over my enemies;
    You disgrace those who hate me.
O God, I give glory to You all day long
    and constantly praise Your name.

But at times I feel like Your people did—

    that You had tossed them aside in dishonor;
    that You stopped leading their armies to battle;
    that You made them retreat from their enemies;
    that You allowed those who hated them
        to plunder their land;
    that You gave them up to be butchered like sheep;
    that You scattered them among the nations;

> *You are my King and my God.*
> *You give me victory.*

that You had sold them—Your precious people—
    for a pittance, making nothing on the sale;
that You had let their neighbors mock them;
that You had allowed them to become an object of scorn
    and derision to those around them;
that You had made them the butt of jokes,
    with those around them shaking their heads
    at them in scorn;
that they could not escape the constant humiliation,
    with shame written across their faces;
that all they heard were the taunts of their mockers;
that all they saw were their vengeful enemies;
that You had crushed them and left them
    in a heap of ruins overrun by wild dogs;
that You had covered them with darkness and death;
    and that they were being killed every day,
    being slaughtered like sheep.

Though I feel like this at times, I have not forgotten You.
I have not violated Your covenant.
My heart has not deserted You.
I have not strayed from Your path.
If I had forgotten Your name
    or spread my hands in prayer to foreign gods,
    You would surely have known it,
    for You know the secrets of every heart.

Wake up, O Lord! Why do You sleep?
Get up! Do not reject me forever.
Why do You look the other way?
Why do You ignore my suffering and oppression?
I collapse in the dust, lying face down in the dirt.
Rise up! Help me!
Redeem me because of Your unfailing love.

You know the secrets of every heart.

45

Beautiful words stir my heart.
I will recite a lovely poem about You, Jesus, the King,
    for my tongue is like the pen of a skillful poet.
Jesus, You are the most handsome of all.
Gracious words stream from Your lips.
The Father Himself has blessed You forever.

Put on Your sword, O mighty warrior!
You are so glorious, so majestic!
In Your majesty, ride out to victory,
    defending truth, humility, and justice.
Go forth to perform awe-inspiring deeds!
Your arrows are sharp, piercing Your enemies' hearts.
The nations fall beneath Your feet.

Your throne endures forever and ever.
You rule with a scepter of justice.
You love justice and hate evil.
Therefore the Father has anointed You, pouring out
    the oil of joy on You more than on anyone else.
Myrrh, aloes, and cassia perfume Your robes.
In ivory palaces the music of strings entertains You.
You allow me to stand by Your side at Your right hand.
You will exalt me, give me honor,
    and adorn me at the proper time.

Jesus:

> *You are the most handsome of all.*
> *You are a mighty warrior.*
> *You defend truth, humility, and justice.*
> *You love justice and hate evil.*
> *You will exalt me.*

Lord, help me to listen to You
     and to take to heart what You say.
Give me the courage to renounce all others
     giving preference to You, over even my family.
As You delight in the beauty of my holiness,
     I will honor You, for You are my Lord.
You will have others shower me with gifts,
     and the wealthy will beg for my favor.

You will make me glorious in the eyes of those around me,
     as You draw me to You.
What a joyful and enthusiastic procession it will be
     when I enter Your palace!

I will carry on Your dynasty.
You will make me a prince throughout the land.
I will bring honor to Your name in every generation.
Therefore, the nations will praise You forever and ever.

Jesus:

*You are worthy of all honor and
praise forever and ever.*

46

You are my refuge and strength,
    always ready to help in times of trouble.
So I will not fear when earthquakes come
    and the mountains crumble into the sea;
    Let the oceans roar and foam.
Let the mountains tremble as the waters surge!

A river brings joy to Your city,
    Your sacred home, O Most High.
You dwell in that city; It cannot be destroyed.
From the very break of day, You will protect it.
The nations are in chaos, and their kingdoms crumble!
Your voice thunders, and the earth melts!
You, the LORD of Heaven's Armies, are here with me;
    You, the God of Israel, are my fortress.

Show me Your glorious works, O LORD.
Show me how You bring destruction upon the world.
You cause wars to end throughout the earth.
You break the bow and snap the spear;
    You burn the shields with fire.

You tell me to be still and know that You are God,
    that You will be exalted among the nations,
    and that You will be exalted in the earth.
You, the LORD of Heaven's Armies, are here with me;
    You, the God of Israel, are my fortress.

> *You are my refuge and strength.*
> *You are here with me.*
> *You are my fortress.*
> *You are God.*
> *You will be exalted among the nations.*
> *You will be exalted in the earth.*

47

I will clap my hands!
And shout to You with joyful praise!
For You, O LORD Most High, are awesome.
You are the great King who rules the whole earth.
You subdue the nations before me,
     putting my enemies beneath my feet.
You chose my inheritance for me.

You ascended with a mighty shout.
You ascended with trumpets blaring.
I will sing praises to You, God, sing praises;
     Sing praises to You, my King, sing praises!
For You are the King over all the earth.
I will praise You with a psalm.

You reign above the nations, sitting on Your holy throne.
The rulers of the world have gathered
     together with Your people.
For all the kings of the earth belong to You.
You are highly exalted.

You are awesome.
You rule the whole earth.

48

How great are You LORD, how deserving of praise,
    in Your city, which sits on Your holy mountain!
It is high and magnificent; The whole earth rejoices to see it!
Mount Zion, the holy mountain,
    is Your city—the city of the great King!
You Yourself are in Jerusalem's towers,
    revealing Yourself as its defender.

The kings of the earth joined forces
    and advanced against the city.
But when they saw it, they were stunned;
    They were terrified and ran away.
They were gripped with terror and writhed in pain
    like a woman in labor.
You destroyed them like the mighty ships of Tarshish
    shattered by a powerful east wind.

I have heard of the city's glory, and long to see it myself—
    Your city—the city of the LORD of Heaven's Armies.
It is Your city, God; You will establish her forever.

O God, I meditate on Your unfailing love as I worship You.
As Your name deserves, O God,
    You will be praised to the ends of the earth.
Your strong right hand is filled with victory.
Let the people on Mount Zion rejoice.
Let all the towns of Judah be glad because of Your justice.

> *You are great.*
> *You deserve all praise.*
> *Your love is unfailing.*

Man can inspect the city of Jerusalem, walk around,
    and count the many towers.
They can take note of the fortified walls
    and tour all the citadels,
    that You may describe them to future generations.
For that is what You are like.

You are my God forever and ever,
    and You will guide me until I die.

You are my God forever and ever.
You are my guide.

49

LORD, I want to tell everyone in the world to pay attention.
The high and low, rich and poor.
I will speak wisdom and share my profound thoughts.
I listen carefully to many proverbs and
    solve riddles with inspiration from music.

Why should I fear when trouble comes,
    when enemies surround me?
They trust in their wealth and boast of great riches.
Yet they cannot redeem themselves from death
    by paying a ransom to You.
You tell me that redemption does not come so easily,
    for no one can ever pay enough
    to live forever and never see the grave.
Those who are wise must finally die,
    just like the foolish and senseless,
    leaving all their wealth behind.

LORD, I know the grave is their eternal home,
    where they will stay forever.
They may name their estates after themselves,
    but their fame will not last.
You tell me they will die, just like animals.
This is the fate of fools,
    though they are remembered as being wise.
Like sheep, they are led to the grave,
    where death will be their shepherd.

You are my Redeemer.

You assure me that, in the morning,
    the godly will rule over them.
Their bodies will rot in the grave, far from their grand estates.
But as for me, God, You will redeem my life.
You will snatch me from the power of the grave.

So, I will not be dismayed when the wicked grow rich
    and their homes become ever more splendid.
For when they die, they take nothing with them.
Their wealth will not follow them into the grave.
In this life, they consider themselves fortunate
    and are applauded for their success.
But they will die like all before them
    and never again see the light of day.
People who boast of their wealth don't understand;
    They will die, just like animals.
But as for me, You will redeem my life
    and snatch me from the power of the grave.

You have power over the grave.

50

You Lord, the Mighty One, are God, and You have spoken.
You have summoned all humanity
    from where the sun rises to where it sets.
From Mount Zion, the perfection of beauty,
    You shine in glorious radiance.
You approach and are not silent.
Fire devours everything in Your way,
    and a great storm rages around You.
You call on the heavens above
    and the earth below to judge Your people.

Lord, call me to You as one of the faithful
    who made a covenant with You by sacrifice.
May the heavens proclaim Your righteousness,
    for You Yourself are judge.
I will listen as You speak.
You are God, my God!

Lord, please take pleasure in my offering—my life.
I know You need nothing I have.
For all the animals of the forest are Yours,
    and You own the cattle on a thousand hills.
You know every bird on the mountains,
    and all the animals of the field are Yours.
If You were hungry, You would have no reason to tell me,
    for all the world is Yours and everything in it.
You don't eat the meat of bulls or drink the blood of goats.

You shine in glorious radiance.
You are not silent.
You need nothing.

Thankfulness is my sacrifice to You, O God.
Give me the strength to fulfill my vows
    to You—the Most High.
I will pray to You when I am in trouble.
For I know You will rescue me and honor me.

LORD, give me a heart that longs:

    To recite Your decrees and obey Your covenant;
    To never refuse Your discipline or
        treat Your words like trash;
    To never approve of thieves or
        spend my time with adulterers;
    To never allow my mouth to be filled with wickedness
        or my tongue to be full of lies; and
    To never sit around and slander
        my brother—my own mother's son.

LORD, if I do any of these things, please do not remain silent.
Do not allow me to think You don't care.
Rebuke me and reveal to me my offenses against You, LORD,
    so that I may confess them and repent;
    And so that I may not forget You and You
    be inclined to tear me apart, with no one to rescue me.

Give me a thankful heart, for You say that
    giving thanks is a sacrifice that truly honors You.
Please teach me to stay on Your path;
    And show me Your salvation.

You will rescue me and honor me.

51

Be gracious to me, O God, according to Your lovingkindness;
   According to the greatness of Your compassion,
   blot out my transgressions.
Wash me thoroughly from my iniquity
   and cleanse me from my sin.
For I know my transgressions, and my sin is ever before me.
Against You, You only, I have sinned
   and done what is evil in Your sight,
   so that You are justified when You speak
   and blameless when You judge.

Behold, I was brought forth in iniquity,
   and in sin my mother conceived me.
Behold, You desire truth in the innermost being,
   and in the hidden part You will make me know wisdom.
Purify me with hyssop, and I shall be clean;
   Wash me, and I shall be whiter than snow.
Make me to hear joy and gladness;
   Let the bones which You have broken rejoice.
Hide Your face from my sins and blot out all my iniquities.

Create in me a clean heart, O God,
   and renew a steadfast spirit within me.
Do not cast me away from Your presence
   and do not take Your Holy Spirit from me.
Restore to me the joy of Your salvation
   and sustain me with a willing spirit.
Then I will teach transgressors Your ways,
   and sinners will be converted to You.

You are justified when You speak.
You are blameless when You judge.
You will make me know wisdom.

Deliver me from bloodguiltiness, O God,
    the God of my salvation;
    Then my tongue will joyfully sing of Your righteousness.
O LORD, open my lips,
    that my mouth may declare Your praise.
For You do not delight in sacrifice, otherwise I would give it;
    You are not pleased with burnt offering.
Your preferred sacrifices are a broken spirit;
    A broken and a contrite heart, O God, You will not despise.

By Your favor, LORD, do good to me;
    Strengthen and protect my family.
Take delight in my righteous sacrifices—
    my broken and contrite heart,
    my confessions, and my repentance.

You do not delight in sacrifice.
You are not pleased with burnt offering.
You delight in a broken spirit and a contrite heart.

52

I will say to the wicked:

"Why do you boast about your crimes?
Don't you realize God's justice continues forever?
All day long you plot destruction.
Your tongue cuts like a sharp razor;
    You're an expert at telling lies.
You love evil more than good
    and lies more than truth.
You love to destroy others with your words, you liar!
But God will strike you down once and for all.
He will pull you from your home
    and uproot you from the land of the living."

The righteous will see this and be amazed.
They will laugh and say:

"Look what happens to men
    who do not trust in God.
They trust their wealth instead
    and grow more and more bold in their wickedness."

But I am like an olive tree, thriving in Your house, O God.
I will always trust in Your unfailing love.
I will praise You forever, O God, for what You have done.
I will trust in Your good name
    in the presence of Your faithful people.

Your justice continues forever.
Your love is unfailing.

53

The fool has said in his heart, "There is no God."
They are corrupt, and their actions are evil;
    Not one of them does good!
You look down from heaven on the entire human race
    to see if anyone is truly wise, if anyone seeks You.
But no, all have turned away; All have become corrupt.

No one does good, not a single one!
Will those who do evil never learn?
They eat up Your people like bread
    and wouldn't think of praying to You.
Terror will grip them,
    terror like they have never known before.
You will scatter the bones of Your enemies.
You will put them to shame, for You have rejected them.

David prayed for the salvation of Israel to come out of Zion,
    restoring Your people and making Israel glad.
I thank you for having done so—in Jesus.

You will scatter the bones of Your enemies.
You brought salvation out of Jerusalem.

54

Come with great power, O God, and rescue me!
Defend me with Your might.
Listen to my prayer, O God.
Pay attention to my plea.
As strangers attacked David
    and violent people tried to kill him,
    I feel like many people are against me,
    and they care nothing for You.

But You are my helper.
You keep me alive!
Make the evil plans of my enemies be turned against them.
In Your faithfulness, deliver me from them.

I will sacrifice a voluntary offering to You;
    I will praise Your name, O LORD, for it is good.
For You have rescued me from my troubles
    and helped me to triumph over my enemies.

You are my helper.
You keep me alive.
Your name is good.
You have rescued me.

55

Listen to my prayer, O God. Do not ignore my cry for help!
Please listen and answer me,
 for I am overwhelmed by my troubles.
My enemies shout at me, making loud and wicked threats.
They bring trouble on me and angrily hunt me down.
My heart pounds in my chest. The terror of death assaults me.
Fear and trembling overwhelm me, and I can't stop shaking.
Oh, that I had wings like a dove;
 Then I would fly away and rest!
I would fly far away to the quiet of the wilderness.
How quickly I would escape—
 far from this wild storm of hatred.

Confuse them, Lord, and frustrate their plans,
 for I see violence and conflict in the city.
Its walls are patrolled day and night against invaders,
 but the real danger is wickedness within the city.
Everything is falling apart;
 Threats and cheating are rampant in the streets.

It is not just an enemy who taunts me—
 I can bear that.
It is not just my foes who so arrogantly insult me—
 I can hide from them.
Instead, at times,
 it is my own close friends who seem to betray me.
What good fellowship I once enjoyed
 as we worshiped You together.
Also, at times, I long for death to stalk my enemies
 and for the grave to swallow them alive,
 for evil makes its home within them.
But I will call on You, God, and You will rescue me.

You will rescue me.

Morning, noon, and night I cry out in my distress,
    and You hear my voice.
You ransom me and keep me safe
    from the battle waged against me,
    though many still oppose me.
You, God, who has ruled forever,
    will hear me and humble them.
For my enemies refuse to change their ways;
    They do not fear You.

I have had friends who have betrayed me
    and have broken promises.
Their words were as smooth as butter,
    but in their hearts was war.
Their words were as soothing as lotion,
    but underneath were daggers!

I give my burdens to You, LORD,
    for I know You will take care of me.
You will not permit the godly to slip and fall.
But You, O God, will send the wicked
    down to the pit of destruction.
Murderers and liars will die young,
    but I am trusting You to save me.

> *You hear my voice.*
> *You ransom me and keep me safe.*
> *You have ruled forever.*
> *You will take care of me.*
> *You will not permit the godly to slip and fall.*
> *You will save me.*

56

O God, have mercy on me, for people are hounding me.
My enemies attack me all day long.
I am constantly hounded by those who slander me,
    and many are boldly attacking me.

But, when I am afraid, I will put my trust in You.
I praise You, God, for what You have promised.
In You, I have put my trust; I shall not be afraid.
What can mere man do to me?

They are always twisting what I say.
They spend their days plotting to harm me.
They come together to spy on me—watching my every step,
    eager to kill me.
Don't let them get away with their wickedness;
    In Your anger, O God, bring them down.

You keep track of all my sorrows.
You put my tears in Your bottle.
You have recorded each one in Your book.

My enemies will turn back when I call to You for help.
This I know, that You are for me.
I praise You, God, for what You have promised.
Yes, Lord, I praise You for what You have promised.
In You, God, I have put my trust, I shall not be afraid.
What can man do to me?

You are for me.
You keep Your promises.

I will fulfill my vows to You, O God;
    I will offer You a sacrifice of thanks.
For You have delivered my soul from death.
You have kept my feet from stumbling.
So, now, I can walk in Your presence,
    O God, in Your life-giving light.

> *You have delivered my soul from death.*
> *You keep my feet from stumbling.*
> *You are worthy of all my trust.*

57

Have mercy on me, O God, have mercy!
I look to You for protection.
I will hide beneath the shadow of Your wings
    until the danger passes by.
I cry out to You, O God Most High,
    to You who will fulfill Your purpose for me.
You will send help from heaven to rescue me,
    disgracing those who hound me.
You will send forth Your unfailing love and faithfulness.
I am surrounded by fierce lions
    who greedily devour human prey—
    whose teeth pierce like spears and arrows,
    and whose tongues cut like swords.
Be exalted, O God, above the highest heavens!
Make Your glory shine over all the earth.
My enemies have set a trap for me.
I am weary from distress.
They have dug a deep pit in my path,
    but they themselves have fallen into it.
My heart is confident in You, O God;
    My heart is confident.
No wonder I can sing Your praises!
I will tell my heart to awaken.
I will get out my instruments.
I will wake the dawn with my song.
I will thank You, Lord, among all the people.
I will sing Your praises among the nations.
For Your unfailing love is as high as the heavens.
Your faithfulness reaches to the clouds.
Be exalted, O God, above the highest heavens.
Make Your glory shine over all the earth.

You will save me from my enemies.
You are worthy of all praise.

58

LORD, the rulers of this world don't know
    the meaning of the word justice.
They do not judge people fairly.
They plot injustice in their hearts
    and spread violence throughout the land.
These wicked people are born sinners;
    Even from birth they have lied and gone their own way.
They spit venom like deadly snakes;
    They are like cobras that refuse to listen,
    ignoring the tunes of the snake charmers,
    no matter how skillfully they play.

Break off their fangs, O God!
Smash the jaws of these lions, O LORD!
David asked You:
    to make them disappear like water into thirsty ground;
    to make their weapons useless in their hands;
    to make them be like snails that dissolve into slime,
        like a stillborn child who will never see the sun;
    and to sweep them away, both young and old,
        faster than a pot heats over burning thorns.

He longed for the day when the godly
    would rejoice at seeing injustice avenged
    and wash their feet in the blood of the wicked.
While David asked You to exact justice on his enemies
    and to destroy them, I ask that You
    open the eyes of the wicked and save them.
But, like David, I look forward to the day when, at last,
    everyone will say,

    "There truly is a reward for those who live for God;
    Surely there is a God who judges justly here on earth."

> *You will judge the earth.*
> *You will bring justice.*

59

Rescue me from my enemies, O God.
Protect me from those who have come to destroy me.
Rescue me from these criminals.
Save me from these murderers.
They have set an ambush for me.
Fierce enemies are out there waiting, LORD,
    though I have not sinned or offended them.
I have done nothing wrong, yet they prepare to attack me.
Wake up! See what is happening and help me!
O LORD, God of Heaven's Armies, the God of Israel,
    wake up and punish those hostile nations.
But, though they are wicked traitors,
    please remove the veil from their eyes, O LORD.

They come out at night, snarling like vicious dogs
    as they prowl the streets.
Listen to the filth that comes from their mouths;
    Their words cut like swords.
"After all, who can hear me?" they sneer.
But LORD, You laugh at them.
You scoff at all the hostile nations.
You are my strength; I wait for You to rescue me,
    for You, O God, are my fortress.
In Your unfailing love, You will stand with me.
You will let me look down in triumph on all my enemies.

> *You scoff at all the hostile nations.*
> *You are my strength, my fortress, and my refuge.*
> *You will rescue me.*
> *You will stand with me.*

Don't kill them, for men soon forget such lessons;
     Stagger them with Your power,
     and bring them to their knees, O LORD, my shield.
Because of the sinful things they say,
     because of the evil that is on their lips,
     let them be captured by their pride,
     their curses, and their lies.

Though I may feel like asking You
     to destroy them in Your anger
     or to wipe them out completely,
     so that the whole world would know that You reign;
     Instead, God, please open their eyes to Your salvation,
     to Your Son.

My enemies come out at night,
     snarling like vicious dogs as they prowl the streets.
They scavenge for food but go to sleep unsatisfied.

But as for me, I will sing about Your power.
Each morning I will sing with joy about Your unfailing love.
For You have been my refuge,
     a place of safety when I am in distress.
O my Strength, to You I sing praises,
     for You, O God, are my refuge,
     the God who shows me unfailing love.

You are my strength.
You show me unfailing love.

60

I feel like You have rejected me, O God, and broken me.
I feel like You have been angry with me.
Restore me to Your favor.
You have shaken the land and split it open.
Seal the cracks, for it trembles.
I feel like You have been very hard on me.
But You have raised a banner for those who fear You—
    a rallying point in the face of attack.
Now rescue me. Save me by Your power, and answer me.
Make promises to me, O LORD,
    like those You made to David,
    when, in Your holiness, You said:

"I WILL DIVIDE UP SHECHEM WITH JOY.
I WILL MEASURE OUT THE VALLEY OF SUCCOTH.
GILEAD IS MINE, AND MANASSEH, TOO.
EPHRAIM, MY HELMET, WILL PRODUCE MY WARRIORS,
AND JUDAH, MY SCEPTER, WILL PRODUCE MY KINGS.
BUT MOAB, MY WASHBASIN, WILL BECOME MY SERVANT,
AND I WILL WIPE MY FEET ON EDOM
AND SHOUT IN TRIUMPH OVER PHILISTIA."

Who will lead me into my next battle?
Who will bring me victory over my next opponent?
Have You rejected me, O God?
Will You no longer go with me?
Oh, please help me against my enemies,
    for all human help is useless.
With Your help I will do mighty things,
    for You will trample down my adversaries.

> *You will lead me.*
> *You will never reject me.*
> *You will enable me to do mighty things.*

61

O God, listen to my cry!
Hear my prayer!
From the ends of the earth, I cry to You for help
    when my heart is overwhelmed.
Lead me to the towering rock of safety,
    for You are my safe refuge,
    a fortress where my enemies cannot reach me.
Let me live forever in Your sanctuary,
    safe beneath the shelter of Your wings!

For You have heard my vows, O God.
You have given me an inheritance
    reserved for those who fear Your name.
Thank You for adding many years to the life of the King.
Thank You for making His years span the generations!
Thank You for revealing to me that He will reign forever.
Watch over Him with Your unfailing love and faithfulness.
I will sing praises to Your name forever
    as I daily worship You with my life.

You are my rock.
You are my safe refuge.
You are a fortress, protecting me from my enemies.
You have given me an inheritance of eternity with You.

62

I wait quietly before You, for my victory comes from You.
You alone are my rock and my salvation,
    my fortress where I will never be shaken.
How long, O Lord, will You allow people to attack me?
To them I'm just a broken-down wall or a tottering fence.
They plan to topple me from my high position.
They delight in telling lies about me.
They praise me to my face but curse me in their hearts.
Let all that I am wait quietly before You,
    for my hope is in You.
You alone are my rock and my salvation,
    my fortress where I will not be shaken.
My victory and honor come from You alone.
You are my refuge, a rock where no enemy can reach me.
I trust in You at all times.
I pour out my heart to You, for You are my refuge.
Common people are as worthless as a puff of wind,
    and the powerful are not what they appear to be.
If I weigh them on the scales,
    together they are lighter than a breath of air.
I will not make my living by extortion
    or put my hope in stealing.
And if my wealth increases,
    I will not make it the center of my life.
You have spoken plainly, and I have heard it many times:
    Power, O God, belongs to You,
    and unfailing love is Yours, O Lord.
Surely You repay all people
    according to what they have done.

> *You alone are my rock and my salvation.*
> *You are my fortress.*
> *You are my refuge.*
> *You repay all people according to what they have done.*

63

O God, You are my God; I earnestly search for You.
My soul thirsts for You; My flesh yearns for You,
   in a dry and weary land where there is no water.

I have seen You in Your sanctuary
   and gazed upon Your power and glory.
Your unfailing love is better than life itself;
   How I praise You!
I will praise You as long as I live,
   lifting up my hands to You in prayer.
You satisfy me more than the richest feast.
I will praise You with songs of joy.
I lie awake thinking of You,
   meditating on You through the night.
Because You are my helper,
   I sing for joy in the shadow of Your wings.
I cling to You; Your strong right hand holds me securely.

But those plotting to destroy me will come to ruin.
They will go down into the depths of the earth.
They will die by the sword and become the food of jackals.
But I will rejoice in You, God.
All who swear by You will glory in You,
   while liars will be silenced.

You are my God.
Your unfailing love is better than life itself.
You hold me securely.

64

O God, listen to my complaint.
Protect my life from my enemies' threats.
Hide me from the plots of this evil mob,
  from this gang of wrongdoers.
They sharpen their tongues like swords
  and aim their bitter words like arrows.
They shoot from ambush at the innocent,
  attacking suddenly and fearlessly.

They encourage each other to do evil
  and plan how to set their traps in secret.
"Who will ever notice?" they ask.
As they plot their crimes, they say,
  "We have devised the perfect plan!"
Yes, the human heart and mind are cunning.

But You, God, will shoot them with Your arrows,
  suddenly striking them down.
Their own tongues will ruin them,
  and all who see them will shake their heads in scorn.
Then everyone will be afraid;
  They will proclaim Your mighty acts
  and realize all the amazing things You do.

The godly will rejoice and find shelter in You, LORD.
And those who do what is right will praise You.

You hear my complaints.
You will bring justice.
You protect me.

65

What mighty praise, O God, belongs to You in Zion.
I will fulfill my vows to You, for You answer my prayers.
I must come to You.
Though I am overwhelmed by my sins, You forgive them all.
What joy for those You choose to bring near,
    those who live in Your holy courts.
What festivities await me inside Your holy temple

You faithfully answer my prayers with awesome deeds,
    O God my savior.
You are the hope of everyone on earth,
    even those who sail on distant seas.
You formed the mountains by Your power
    and armed Yourself with mighty strength.
You quieted the raging oceans with their pounding waves
    and silenced the shouting of the nations.
Those who live at the ends of the earth
    stand in awe of Your wonders.
From where the sun rises to where it sets,
    You inspire shouts of joy.

You answer my prayers.
You forgive my sins.
You are my savior.
You are the hope of everyone on earth.
You formed the mountains by Your power.
You inspire shouts of joy.

You take care of the earth and water it,
    making it rich and fertile.
The river of God has plenty of water;
    It provides a bountiful harvest of grain,
    for You have ordered it so.
You drench the plowed ground with rain,
    melting the clods and leveling the ridges.
You soften the earth with showers
    and bless its abundant crops.
You crown the year with a bountiful harvest;
    Even the hard pathways overflow with abundance.
The grasslands of the wilderness become a lush pasture,
    and the hillsides blossom with joy.
The meadows are clothed with flocks of sheep,
    and the valleys are carpeted with grain.
They all shout and sing for joy!

You take care of the earth.

66

I will shout joyful praises to You, O God!
I will sing about the glory of Your name!
I will tell the world how glorious You are.
How awesome are Your deeds!
Your enemies cringe before Your mighty power.
Everything on earth will worship You;
> They will sing Your praises,
>> shouting Your name in glorious songs.

I will tell others to come and see what You have done,
> what awesome miracles You perform for people.
You made a dry path through the Red Sea,
> and Your people went across on foot.
I rejoice in You.
For by Your great power You rule forever.
You watch every movement of the nations;
> Lord, do not let the rebellious exalt themselves.

Let the whole world bless You, my God,
> and loudly sing Your praises.
My life is in Your hands,
> and You keep my feet from stumbling.
You have tested me, O God;
> You have purified me like silver.
You captured me in Your net
> and laid the burden of slavery on my back.
Then You put a leader over me.
I went through fire and flood,
> but You brought me to a place of great abundance.

Your deeds are awesome.
You keep my feet from stumbling.
You have purified me like silver.

The psalmist promised to enter Your temple
  with burnt offerings,
    and to fulfill the vows he had made to You—
    the sacred vows that he made when he was in deep trouble.
He promised to sacrifice burnt offerings to You—
    the best of his rams as a pleasing aroma,
    and a sacrifice of bulls and male goats.
With the same heart, Lord, I come before You,
    with a broken and contrite heart, offering You my life.

I will tell those who fear You to come and listen.
I will tell them what You have done for me.
For I cried out to You for help, praising You as I spoke.
If I had not confessed the sin in my heart,
    You would not have listened.
But You did listen! You paid attention to my prayer.
I praise You, God, for You did not ignore my prayer
    or withdraw Your unfailing love from me.

You pay attention to my prayers.
You love me perpetually.

67

God, be merciful and bless me.
Make Your face smile with favor on me,
     that Your way may be known throughout the earth,
     Your salvation among all nations.

Let the nations praise You, O God.
Yes, let all the nations praise You.
Let the whole world sing for joy,
     because You govern the nations with justice
     and guide the people of the whole world.

Let the nations praise You, O God.
Yes, let all the nations praise You.
The earth has yielded its harvest,
     and You, God, my God, richly bless me.
Yes, You bless me,
     that people all over the world may fear You.

You govern the nations with justice.
You bless me.

68

David asked You to rise up and scatter Your enemies,
    that those who hate You would run for their lives.
He asked You to blow them away like smoke,
    to melt them like wax in a fire,
    and to let the wicked perish in Your presence.
But I will rejoice. I will be glad in Your presence.
I will be filled with joy.
I will sing praises to You and to Your name!
I will sing loud praises to You who rides the clouds.
Your name is the LORD—I will rejoice in Your presence!

Father to the fatherless, defender of widows—
    You are God, whose dwelling is holy.
You place the lonely in families;
    You set the prisoners free and give them joy.
But You make the rebellious live in a sun-scorched land.

O God, when You led Your people out from Egypt,
    when You marched through the dry wasteland,
    the earth trembled,
    and the heavens poured down rain before You,
    the God of Sinai, before You, the God of Israel.
You sent abundant rain, O God, to refresh the weary land.
There Your people finally settled,
    and with a bountiful harvest, O God,
    You provided for Your needy people.

Your name is the LORD.
You set the prisoners free.

You give the word, and a great army brings the good news.
Enemy kings and their armies flee,
>   while women divide the plunder.
Even those who lived among the sheepfolds
>   found treasures—doves with wings of silver
>   and feathers of gold.
You scattered the enemy kings
>   like a blowing snowstorm on Mount Zalmon.

The mountains of Bashan are majestic,
>   with many peaks stretching high into the sky.
And yet they look with envy at the mountain
>   where You chose to live.
Surrounded by unnumbered thousands of chariots,
>   You came from Mount Sinai into Your sanctuary.
When You ascended to the heights,
>   You led a crowd of captives.
You received gifts from the people,
>   even from those who rebelled against You.
Then You dwelt among them there.

I praise You, LORD; For You are my Savior!
For each day You carry me in Your arms.
You are a God who saves—the Sovereign LORD
>   who rescues me from death.
But You will smash the heads of Your enemies,
>   crushing the skulls of those who love their guilty ways.
You assured David, saying:
>   "I will bring my enemies down from Bashan;
>   >   I will bring them up from the depths of the sea.
>   You, my child, will wash your feet in their blood,
>   >   and even your dogs will get their share!"

You are my Savior.
You carry me in Your arms.
You rescue me from death.

Your procession has come into view, O God—
    the procession of my God and King
    as You go into the sanctuary.
Singers are in front, musicians behind;
    Between them are young women playing tambourines.
I will praise You, God; For You are the source of life.
In Your procession, the little tribe of Benjamin leads the way.
Then comes a great throng of rulers from Judah
    and all the rulers of Zebulun and Naphtali.

Summon Your might, O God.
Display Your power, O God, as You have in the past.
The kings of the earth are bringing tribute to You.
Rebuke these enemy nations—
    these wild animals lurking in the reeds,
    this herd of bulls among the weaker calves.
Make them bring bars of silver in humble tribute.
Scatter the nations that delight in war.
Let Egypt come with gifts of precious metals;
    Let Ethiopia bring tribute to You.
I will sing to You, God. I will sing praises to You.
I will sing to You who rides across the ancient heavens,
    Your mighty voice thundering from the sky.
I will tell everyone about Your power.
Your majesty shines down on Your people;
    Your strength is mighty in the heavens.
You are awesome in Your sanctuary.
You give power and strength to Your people.

Praise be to You, O God!

You are the source of life.
You give power and strength to Your people.

69

Save me, O God, for the floodwaters are up to my neck.
Deeper and deeper I sink into the mire; I can't find a foothold.
I am in deep water, and the floods overwhelm me.
I am exhausted from crying for help; My throat is parched.
My eyes are swollen with weeping,
     waiting for You, my God, to help me.
Those who hate me without cause
     outnumber the hairs on my head.
Many enemies try to destroy me with lies,
     demanding that I give back what I didn't steal.

O God, You know how foolish I am;
     My sins cannot be hidden from You.
Don't let those who trust in You be ashamed because of me,
     O Sovereign LORD of Heaven's Armies.
Don't let me cause them to be humiliated, O God of Israel.
For I endure insults for Your sake;
     Humiliation is written all over my face.
Even my own sisters pretend they don't know me;
     They treat me like a stranger.

LORD, give me a passion for Your house that consumes me,
And, should the insults of those who insult You fall on me,
     LORD, give me the faith I need to endure.
When I weep and fast and feel like those around me
     are scoffing at me, or when I appropriately show sorrow
     and feel like those around me are making fun of me, or
     when I feel like everyone around me is gossiping about me,
     LORD, give me wisdom to trust in You more.

You know me.
You give me faith.

I will keep praying to You, Lord,
    hoping You will show me favor.
In Your unfailing love, O God,
    answer my prayer with Your sure salvation.
Rescue me from the mud; Don't let me sink any deeper!
Save me from those who hate me,
    and pull me from these deep waters.
Don't let the floods overwhelm me,
    or the deep waters swallow me,
    or the pit of death devour me.

Answer my prayers, O Lord,
    for Your unfailing love is wonderful.
Take care of me, for Your mercy is so plentiful.
Don't hide from Your servant;
    Answer me quickly, for I am in deep trouble!
Come and redeem me; Free me from my enemies.

You know of my shame, scorn, and disgrace.
You see all that my enemies are doing.
Their insults have broken my heart, and I am in despair.
If only one person would show some pity;
    If only one would turn and comfort me.
But instead, like David, I feel like they are out to get me.

Your love is unfailing.
Your salvation is sure.
Your unfailing love is wonderful.
Your mercy is plentiful.

At times, I confess, I am inclined to pray, as David did:

"Let the bountiful table set before them
    become a snare and their prosperity become a trap.
Let their eyes go blind so they cannot see,
    and make their bodies shake continually.
Pour out Your fury on them;
    Consume them with Your burning anger.
Let their homes become desolate
    and their tents be deserted.
To the one You have punished,
    they add insult to injury;
    They add to the pain of those You have hurt.
Pile their sins up high, and don't let them go free.
Erase their names from the Book of Life;
    Don't let them be counted among the righteous."

I am suffering and in pain.
Rescue me, O God, by Your saving power.
I will praise Your name with singing,
    and I will honor You with thanksgiving.
For this will please You more than sacrificing cattle,
    more than presenting a bull with its horns and hooves.
The humble will see You at work and be glad.
Let all who seek Your help be encouraged.
For You hear the cries of the needy;
    You do not despise Your imprisoned people.
I will praise You, as will all heaven and earth,
    and the seas and all that move in them.
For You will save Jerusalem and rebuild the towns of Judah.
Your people will live there and settle in their own land.
The descendants of those who obey You will inherit the land,
    and those who love You will live there in safety.

You are my rescuer.
You hear the cries of the needy.

70

Please, God, rescue me! Come quickly, LORD, and help me.
Make those who try to kill me be humiliated
    and put to shame.
Make those who take delight in my trouble
    be turned back in disgrace.
Let them be horrified by their shame,
    for they said, "Aha! We've got her now!"

But make all who search for You
    be filled with joy and gladness in You.
Make those who love Your salvation
    repeatedly shout, "God is great!"
But as for me, I am poor and needy;
    Please hurry to my aid, O God.

You are my helper and my savior; O LORD, do not delay.

You are my helper.
You are my savior.

71

O Lord, I have come to You for protection;
    Don't let me be disgraced.
Save me and rescue me, for You do what is right.
Turn Your ear to listen to me, and set me free.
Be my rock of safety where I can always hide.
Give the order to save me,
    for You are my rock and my fortress.
My God, rescue me from the power of the wicked,
    from the clutches of cruel oppressors.
O Lord, You alone are my hope.
I've trusted You, O Lord, from childhood.
Yes, You have been with me from birth;
    From my mother's womb You have cared for me.
No wonder I am always praising You!

My life is an example to many,
    because You have been my strength and protection.
That is why I can never stop praising You;
    I declare Your glory all day long.
Don't set me aside when I get old.
Don't abandon me when my strength is failing.
I feel like my enemies are whispering against me,
    like they are plotting together to kill me,
        saying, "God has abandoned her. Let's go and get her,
    for no one will help her now."

You do what is right.
You are my rock and my fortress.
You alone are my hope.
You have cared for me from birth.

O God, don't stay away. My God, please hurry to help me.
Bring disgrace on my accusers and destruction to their plans.
Humiliate and shame those who want to harm me.
But I will keep on hoping for Your help;
    I will praise You more and more.
I will tell everyone about Your righteousness.
All day long I will proclaim Your saving power,
    though I am not skilled with words.
I will praise Your mighty deeds, O Sovereign LORD.
I will tell everyone that You alone are just.

O God, You have taught me from my earliest childhood,
    and I constantly tell others
    about the wonderful things You do.
When I get old and gray, do not abandon me, O God.
Let me proclaim Your power to this new generation,
    Your mighty miracles to all who come after me.

Your righteousness, O God, reaches to the highest heavens.
You have done such wonderful things.
Who can compare with You, O God?
You have allowed me to suffer much hardship,
    but You will restore me to life again
    and lift me up from the depths of the earth.
You will restore me to even greater honor
    and comfort me once again.

You alone are just.
You will restore me.

Then I will praise You with music,
    because You are faithful to Your promises, O my God.
I will sing praises to You, O Holy One of Israel.
I will shout for joy and sing Your praises,
    for You have ransomed me.
I will tell about Your righteous deeds all day long,
    for everyone who tried to hurt me
    has been shamed and humiliated.

You are faithful to Your promises.
You have ransomed me.

72

Give Your love of justice and righteousness
   to Your Son, O God.
Help Him judge Your people in the right way,
   with the poor always being treated with justice.
May the mountains yield prosperity for all,
   and may the hills be fruitful.
Help Him to defend the poor,
   rescue the children of the needy,
   and crush their oppressors.
May they fear You as long as the sun shines,
   as long as the moon remains in the sky.
Yes, forever!

When He comes down like spring rain
   on freshly cut grass,
   like the showers that water the earth,
   may all the godly flourish during His reign.

Make there be abundant prosperity until the moon is no more.
He will reign from sea to sea,
   and from the Euphrates River to the ends of the earth.
Desert nomads will bow before Him;
   His enemies will fall before Him in the dust.
The western kings of Tarshish
   and other distant lands will bring Him tribute.
The eastern kings of Sheba and Seba will bring Him gifts.
All kings will bow before Him,
   and all nations will serve Him.

Your Son will rule all.

He will rescue the poor when they cry to Him;
    He will help the oppressed,
    who have no one to defend them.
He feels pity for the weak and the needy,
    and He will rescue them.
He will redeem them from oppression and violence,
    for their lives are precious to Him.

Long live the King! May the gold of Sheba be given to Him.
May the people always pray for Him
    and bless Him all day long.
May there be abundant grain throughout the land,
    flourishing even on the hilltops.
May the fruit trees flourish like the cedars of Lebanon,
    and may the people thrive like grass in a field.
The King's name will endure forever;
    It will continue as long as the sun shines.
All nations will be blessed through Him
    and will bring Him praise.

I praise You, LORD God, the God of Israel,
    who alone does such wonderful things.
I praise Your glorious name forever!
May the whole earth be filled with Your glory.
Amen and amen!

> *You defend the poor.*
> *You rescue the children of the needy.*
> *You crush the oppressor.*
> *Your name will endure forever.*

73

Truly You are good to Your people,
 to those whose hearts are pure.
But as for me, I almost lost my footing.
My feet almost slipped out from under me.
For I envied the proud
 when I saw them prosper despite their wickedness.
They seem to live such painless lives;
 Their bodies are so healthy and strong.
They don't have troubles like other people;
 They're not plagued with problems like everyone else.
Arrogance is their necklace and violence their clothing.
Their eyes bulge with abundance;
 They have everything their hearts could ever wish for!
They scoff and speak only evil;
 In their pride they seek to crush others.
They boast against the very heavens,
 and their words strut throughout the earth.
And so the people are dismayed and confused,
 drinking in all their words.
"What does God know?" they ask.
"Does the Most High even know what's happening?"
Look at these wicked people—
 enjoying a life of ease while their riches multiply.

Did I keep my heart pure for nothing?
Did I keep myself innocent for no reason?
I get nothing but trouble all day long;
 Every morning brings me pain.
If I had really spoken this way to others,
 I would have been a traitor to Your people.
So I tried to understand why the wicked prosper.
But what a difficult task it is!

You will judge the wicked.

Then I went into Your sanctuary, O God,
  and I finally understood the destiny of the wicked.
Truly, You put them on a slippery path
  and send them sliding over the cliff to destruction.
In an instant they are destroyed,
  completely swept away by terrors.
When You arise, O Lord,
  You will laugh at their silly ideas
  as a person laughs at dreams in the morning.

Then I realized that my heart was bitter,
  and I was all torn up inside.
I was so foolish and ignorant—
  I must have seemed like a senseless animal to You.
Yet I still belong to You; You hold my right hand.
You guide me with Your counsel,
  leading me to a glorious destiny.
Whom have I in heaven but You?
And besides You, I desire nothing on earth.
My flesh and my heart may fail,
  but You are the strength of my heart
  and my portion forever.

Those who desert You will perish,
  for You destroy those who abandon You.
But as for me, how good it is to be near You!
I have made You my refuge,
  and I will tell everyone about the wonderful things You do.

You are my guide.
You are my heart's desire.
You are my refuge.

74

O God, why does it feel like
>You have rejected me for so long?

Why does Your anger seem so intense against me?

Remember that I am Yours and that You chose me long ago,
>redeemed as Your own special possession!

Remember me like You remembered Jerusalem,
>Your home here on earth,
>when it was laid to ruins
>after the enemy destroyed Your sanctuary.

There Your enemies shouted their victorious battle cries;
>There they set up their battle standards.

They swung their axes like woodcutters in a forest.

With axes and picks, they smashed the carved paneling.

They burned Your sanctuary to the ground.

They defiled the place that bears Your name.

Then they thought, "Let's destroy everything!"

So they burned down all the places
>where You were worshiped.

At times I feel as though
>I no longer see Your miraculous signs.

All the prophets are gone,
>and no one can tell me when it will end.

How long, O God, will You allow my enemies to insult You?

Will You let them dishonor Your name forever?

Why do You hold back Your strong right hand?

At times I long for You to unleash Your powerful fist
>and destroy them;
>But I know that You call me to love them
>and pray for them.

You chose me long ago.

You, O God, are my king from ages past,
    bringing salvation to the earth.
You split the sea by Your strength
    and smashed the heads of the sea monsters.
You crushed the heads of Leviathan
    and let the desert animals eat him.
You caused the springs and streams to gush forth,
    and You dried up rivers that never run dry.
Both day and night belong to You;
    You made the starlight and the sun.
You set the boundaries of the earth,
    and You made both summer and winter.
See how these enemies insult You, LORD.
A foolish nation has dishonored Your name.
Don't let these wild beasts destroy Your turtledoves.
Don't forget Your suffering people forever.

Remember Your covenant promises,
    for the land is full of darkness and violence!
Don't let the downtrodden be humiliated again.
Instead, let the poor and needy praise Your name.

Arise, O God, and defend Your cause.
Remember how these fools insult You all day long.
Don't overlook what Your enemies have said
    or their growing uproar.

You are my king.
You bring salvation to the earth.
You rule over all nature.
You created everything.

75

I give thanks to You, O God!
I give thanks because You are near.
Men declare Your wondrous works.

You have said:

> "At the time I have planned,
>   I will bring justice against the wicked.
> When the earth quakes and its people live in turmoil,
>   I am the one who keeps its foundations firm.
> I warned the proud, 'Stop your boasting!'
> I told the wicked, 'Don't raise your fists!
> Don't raise your fists in defiance at the heavens
>   or speak with such arrogance.'"

For no one on earth—from east or west,
    or even from the wilderness—should raise a defiant fist.
But You alone are the judge;
    You put down one and exalt another.
For You, Lord, hold a cup in Your hand
    that is full of foaming wine mixed with spices.
You pour out the wine in judgment,
    and all the wicked must drink it, draining it to the dregs.

But as for me, I will always proclaim what You have done;
    I will sing praises to You, the God of Jacob.
For You say, "I will break the strength of the wicked,
    but I will increase the power of the godly."

You are near.
You will bring justice to the wicked.
You alone are judge.

76

You were honored in Judah; Your name was great in Israel.
Jerusalem is where You chose to live;
> Mount Zion is what You called Your home.
There You broke fiery arrows of the enemy
> and the shields and swords and weapons of war.

You are resplendent,
> more majestic than the mountains of prey.
Israel's boldest enemies were plundered.
They slept their last sleep.
No warrior could lift a hand against Your people.
At Your rebuke, O God of Jacob,
> their horses and chariots lay still.

No wonder You are greatly feared!
Who can stand before You when Your anger explodes?
From heaven You sentenced Your enemies;
> The earth trembled and stood silent before You.
You stand up to judge those who do evil, O God,
> and to rescue the oppressed of the earth.
Human defiance only enhances Your glory,
> for You use it as a weapon.

I will make vows to You, O Lord, my God,
> and I will keep them.
Let everyone bring tribute to You, the One to be feared.
For You break the spirit of rulers,
> and the kings of the earth fear You.

Your name is great.
You are resplendent.
You judge those who do evil.
You are to be feared.
You break the spirit of rulers.

77

I cry out to You; Yes, I shout.
Oh, that You would listen to me!
When I was in deep trouble, I searched for You, LORD.
All night long I prayed, with hands lifted toward heaven,
    but my soul was not comforted.
I think of You, God, and I moan,
    overwhelmed with longing for Your help.

You don't let me sleep. I am too distressed even to pray!
I think of the good old days, long since ended,
    when my nights were filled with joyful songs.
I search my soul and ponder the difference now.
Have You rejected me forever?
Will You never again be kind to me?
Is Your unfailing love gone forever?
Have Your promises permanently failed?
Have You forgotten to be gracious?
Have You slammed the door on Your compassion?
And I said, "This is my fate;
    The Most High has turned His hand against me."
But then I recall all You have done, O LORD;
    I remember Your wonderful deeds of long ago.
They are constantly in my thoughts.
I cannot stop thinking about Your mighty works.

O God, Your ways are holy.
Is there any god as mighty as You?
You are the God of great wonders!
You demonstrate Your awesome power among the nations.

Your ways are holy.
You are the God of great wonders.

By Your strong arm, You redeemed Your people,
    the descendants of Jacob and Joseph.
When the Red Sea saw You, O God,
    its waters looked and trembled!
The sea quaked to its very depths.
The clouds poured down rain;
    The thunder rumbled in the sky.

Your arrows of lightning flashed.
Your thunder roared from the whirlwind;
    The lightning lit up the world!
The earth trembled and shook.
Your road led through the sea,
    Your pathway through the mighty waters—
    a pathway no one knew was there!
You led Your people along that road like a flock of sheep,
    with Moses and Aaron as their shepherds.

You redeem Your people.

78

I will listen to Your truth, Your words, Your sayings of old,
    which have been passed down for generations.
I will teach others hidden lessons from the past—
    I will not hide these truths from my children
    but will tell the next generation
    about Your glorious deeds,
    about Your power and Your mighty wonders.
For You issued Your laws to Jacob;
    You gave Your instructions to Israel.

You commanded my ancestors to teach them to their children,
    so the next generation might know them—
    even the children not yet born—
    and they in turn will teach their own children.
So each generation should put its confidence in You
    and not forget Your glorious miracles
    but obey Your commands.
Then they will not be like their ancestors—
    stubborn, rebellious, and unfaithful,
    refusing to give their hearts to You.

The warriors of Ephraim, though armed with bows,
    turned their backs and fled on the day of battle.
They did not keep Your covenant
    and refused to live by Your instructions.
They forgot what You had done—
    the great wonders You had shown them,
    the miracles You did for their ancestors
    on the plain of Zoan in the land of Egypt.

You've done great and miraculous things throughout history.

For You divided the sea and led them through,
    making the water stand up like walls!
In the daytime, You led them by a cloud,
    and all night by a pillar of fire.
You split open the rocks in the wilderness
    to give them water, as from a gushing spring.
You made streams pour from the rock,
    making the waters flow down like a river!

Yet they kept on sinning against You,
    rebelling against You, the Most High in the desert.
They stubbornly tested You in their hearts,
    demanding the foods they craved.
They even spoke against You, saying:
    "God can't give me food in the wilderness.
    Yes, He can strike a rock so water gushes out,
        but He can't give his people bread and meat."

When You heard them, You were furious.
The fire of Your wrath burned against Jacob.
Yes, Your anger rose against Israel,
    for they did not believe You or trust You to care for them.
But You commanded the skies to open;
    You opened the doors of heaven.
You rained down manna for them to eat;
    You gave them bread from heaven.
They ate the food of angels!
You gave them all they could hold.
You released the east wind in the heavens
    and guided the south wind by Your mighty power.

You've done great and miraculous things throughout history.

You rained down meat as thick as dust—
    birds as plentiful as the sand on the seashore!
You caused the birds to fall within their camp
    and all around their tents.
The people ate their fill. You gave them what they craved.
But before they satisfied their craving,
    while the meat was yet in their mouths,
Your anger rose against them,
    and You killed their strongest men.
You struck down the finest of Israel's young men.

But in spite of this, the people kept sinning.
Despite Your wonders, they refused to trust You.
So You ended their lives in failure, their years in terror.
When You began killing them, they finally sought You.
They repented and took You seriously.
Then they remembered that You were their rock,
    that You were their redeemer.
But all they gave You was lip service;
    They lied to You with their tongues.

Their hearts were not loyal to You.
They did not keep Your covenant.
Yet You were merciful and forgave their sins
    and did not destroy them all.
Many times You held back Your anger
    and did not unleash Your fury!
For You remembered that they were merely mortal,
    gone like a breath of wind that never returns.

You've done great and miraculous things throughout history.

How often they rebelled against You in the wilderness
    and grieved Your heart in that dry wasteland.
Again and again they tested Your patience
    and provoked You, the Holy One of Israel.
They did not remember Your power
    and how You rescued them from their enemies.

They did not remember Your miraculous signs in Egypt,
    Your wonders on the plain of Zoan.
For You turned their rivers into blood,
    so no one could drink from the streams.
You sent vast swarms of flies to consume them
    and hordes of frogs to ruin them.
You gave their crops to caterpillars;
    Their harvest was consumed by locusts.
You destroyed their grapevines with hail
    and shattered their sycamore-figs with sleet.
You abandoned their cattle to the hail,
    their livestock to bolts of lightning.
You loosed on them Your fierce anger—
    all Your fury, rage, and hostility.
You dispatched against them a band of destroying angels.
You turned Your anger against them;
    You did not spare the Egyptians' lives
    but ravaged them with the plague.
You killed the oldest son in each Egyptian family,
    the flower of youth throughout the land of Egypt.

You've done great and miraculous things throughout history.

But You led Your own people like a flock of sheep,
    guiding them safely through the wilderness.
You kept them safe so they were not afraid;
    But the sea covered their enemies.
You brought them to the border of Your holy land,
    to this land of hills You had won for them.
You drove out the nations before them;
    You gave them their inheritance by lot.
You settled the tribes of Israel into their homes.

But they kept testing and rebelling against You,
    the Most High God. They did not obey Your laws.
They turned back and were as faithless as their parents.
They were as undependable as a crooked bow.
They angered You by building shrines to other gods;
    They made You jealous with their idols.
When You heard them, You were very angry,
    and You completely rejected Israel.
Then You abandoned Your dwelling at Shiloh,
    the Tabernacle where You had lived among the people.

You allowed the Ark of Your might to be captured;
    You surrendered Your glory into enemy hands.
You gave Your people over to be butchered by the sword,
    because You were so angry with Your own people—
    Your special possession.
Their young men were killed by fire;
    Their young women died
    before singing their wedding songs.
Their priests were slaughtered,
    and their widows could not mourn their deaths.

> *You've done great and miraculous things throughout history.*

Then You rose up as though waking from sleep,
  like a warrior aroused from a drunken stupor.
You routed Your enemies and sent them to eternal shame.
But You rejected Joseph's descendants;
  You did not choose the tribe of Ephraim.
You chose instead the tribe of Judah,
  and Mount Zion, which You loved.

There You built Your sanctuary as high as the heavens,
  as solid and enduring as the earth.
You chose Your servant David,
  calling him from the sheep pens.
You took David from tending the ewes and lambs
  and made him the shepherd of Jacob's descendants—
  Your own people, Israel.
You cared for them with a true heart
  and led them with skillful hands.

You've done great and miraculous things throughout history.

79

O God, pagan nations conquered Your land,
Your special possession.
They defiled Your holy temple
and made Jerusalem a heap of ruins.
They left the bodies of Your servants
as food for the birds of heaven.
The flesh of Your godly ones
became food for the wild animals.
Blood flowed like water all around Jerusalem;
No one was left to bury the dead.
Your people were mocked by their neighbors,
making them feel like objects of scorn and derision
to those around them.

O Lord, at times I feel the same way and want to ask:

"How long will You be angry with me? Forever?
How long will Your jealousy burn like fire?"

At times, I wish You would pour out Your wrath
on nations that refuse to acknowledge You—
on kingdoms that do not call upon Your name.
For they devoured Your people Israel,
making the land a desolate wilderness.

Do not hold me guilty for the sins of my ancestors!
Let Your compassion quickly meet my needs,
for I am on the brink of despair.
Help me, O God of my salvation!
Help me for the glory of Your name.
Save me and forgive my sins for the honor of Your name.

*You are patient, not wanting any to perish
but for all to come to repentance.*

Why should pagan nations be allowed to scoff,
asking, "Where is their God?"
I confess, I want to see Your vengeance against the nations,
for they have spilled the blood of Your servants.
Listen to the moaning of the prisoners.
Demonstrate Your great power
by saving those condemned to die.

O Lord, I long to see Your justice,
for you to pay back such nations seven times
for the scorn they have hurled at You.
Then I, Your child, a sheep of Your pasture,
will thank You forever and ever,
praising Your greatness from generation to generation.

You are patient, not wanting any to perish
but for all to come to repentance.

80

Please listen, O Shepherd of Israel,
    You who lead Your people like a flock.
O God, enthroned above the cherubim,
    display Your radiant glory
    to Ephraim, Benjamin, and Manasseh.
Show me Your mighty power.
Come to rescue me!

Turn me again to Yourself, O God.
Make Your face shine down upon me.
Only then will I be saved.
O LORD God of Heaven's Armies,
    at times I feel like You are angry with my prayers.
I feel like You have fed me with sorrow
    and made me drink tears by the bucketful.
I feel like You have made me the scorn of neighbors
    and like my enemies treat me as a joke.

Turn me again to Yourself, O God of Heaven's Armies.
Make Your face shine down upon me.
Only then will I be saved.
You brought Your people from Egypt like a grapevine;
    You drove away the pagan nations and planted it.
You cleared the ground before it,
    and it took root and filled the land.
The mountains were covered with its shadow,
    and its branches covered the mighty cedars.
It spread its branches west to the Mediterranean Sea
    and its shoots east to the Euphrates River.

You lead Your people.
You are enthroned above the cherubim.

But then, You broke down its walls
　　so that all who passed by could steal its fruit. Why?
The wild boar from the forest could devour it,
　　and the wild animals could feed on it.
At times, I feel just like this—
　　like You prepared a wonderful place for me,
　　set me up for success, then pulled back,
　　leaving me exposed.

Come back, I beg You, O God of Heaven's Armies.
Look down from heaven and see my plight.
Care for this grapevine that You Yourself have planted,
　　and for the son You have strengthened for Yourself.
For I feel chopped up and burned by my enemies.
I confess that, at times, I wish they would perish
　　at the sight of Your frown.
Strengthen the man of Your right hand,
　　the son of man whom You made strong for Yourself.
Then I will never abandon You again.
Revive me so I can call on Your name once more.

Turn me again to Yourself, O Lord God of Heaven's Armies.
Make Your face shine down upon me.
Only then will I be saved.

> *You are the God of heaven's armies.*
> *You are my only means of salvation.*

81

I will sing praises to You, O God, my strength.
I will sing to You, the God of Jacob.
You commanded Your people:
    to sing and play the tambourine,
    to play the sweet lyre and the harp,
    to blow the ram's horn at new moon,
    and again at full moon to call a festival!

For this was required by the decrees of Israel;
    It was a regulation of Yours, O God of Jacob.
You made it a law for Israel
    when You attacked Egypt to set them free.

You told Your people, in an unknown voice:

    "Now I will take the load from your shoulders;
        I will free your hands from their heavy tasks.
    You cried to Me in trouble, and I saved you;
        I answered out of the thundercloud
        and tested your faith
        when there was no water at Meribah.

    Listen to Me, O My people,
        while I give you stern warnings.
    O Israel, if you would only listen to Me!
    You must never have a foreign god;
        You must not bow down before a false god.
    For it was I, the Lord your God,
        who rescued you from the land of Egypt.
    Open your mouth wide,
        and I will fill it with good things.

You are my strength.

But no, My people wouldn't listen.
Israel did not want Me around.
So I let them follow their own stubborn desires,
    living according to their own ideas.
Oh, that My people would listen to Me.
Oh, that Israel would follow Me and walk in My paths.
How quickly I would then subdue their enemies.
How soon My hands would be upon their foes.
Those who hate Me would cringe before Me;
    They would be doomed forever.
But I would feed you with the finest wheat.
I would satisfy you with wild honey from the rock."

Speak to me, LORD; For I long to listen to You.

You are the giver of good things.

82

You preside over heaven's court.
You pronounce judgment on the heavenly beings.
How long will You hand down seemingly unjust decisions
    by favoring the wicked?

Give justice to the poor and the orphan;
    Uphold the rights of the oppressed and the destitute.
Rescue the poor and helpless;
    Deliver them from the grasp of evil people.

But these oppressors know nothing; They are so ignorant!
They wander about in darkness,
    while the whole world is shaken to the core.
You called Your people gods,
    as they were children of the Most High.
But You reminded them that they would die
    like all other mere mortals.

Rise up, O God, and judge the earth,
    for all the nations belong to You.

You rule over everything.
You care for the poor and the orphan.

83

O God, do not be silent!
Do not be deaf.
Do not be quiet, O God.
Don't You hear the uproar of Your enemies?
Don't You see that Your arrogant enemies are rising up?
They devise crafty schemes against Your people;
> They conspire against Your precious ones.

"Come," they say, "let me wipe out Israel as a nation.
> We will destroy the very memory of its existence."
Yes, this was their unanimous decision.
They signed a treaty as allies against You—
> the Edomites and Ishmaelites; Moabites and Hagrites;
> Gebalites, Ammonites, and Amalekites;
> and people from Philistia and Tyre.
Assyria joined them, too,
> and allied with the descendants of Lot.

At times I want You to do to those
> who terrorize Your people as You did to the Midianites
> and as You did to Sisera and Jabin at the Kishon River.
They were destroyed at Endor,
> and their decaying corpses fertilized the soil.
At times I want their mighty nobles to die
> as Oreb and Zeeb did;
> And for all their princes to die like Zebah and Zalmunna.
For they said, "Let me seize for my own use
> these pasturelands of God!"

You avenge Your people.

O my God, scatter them like tumbleweed,
    like chaff before the wind!
As a fire burns a forest and as a flame sets mountains ablaze,
    chase them with Your fierce storm;
      Terrify them with Your tempest.
Utterly disgrace them
    until they submit to Your name, O LORD.
Though I want them to be ashamed and terrified forever
    and to die in disgrace, save them LORD.
Then the world will learn that You alone are called the LORD,
    that You alone are the Most High,
      supreme over all the earth.

You alone are the LORD Most High.

84

How lovely is Your dwelling place,
    O Lord of Heaven's Armies.
My soul longed and even yearned for Your courts.
With my whole being, body and soul,
    I will shout joyfully to You, the living God.
Even the sparrow finds a home,
    and the swallow builds her nest
    and raises her young at a place near Your altar,
    O Lord of Heaven's Armies, my King and my God!

What joy for those who can live in Your house,
    always singing Your praises.
What joy for those whose strength comes from You, O Lord,
    who have set their minds on their journey with You.
When they walk through the Valley of Weeping,
    it will become a place of refreshing springs.
The autumn rains will clothe it with blessings.
They will continue to grow stronger,
    and each of them will appear before You.

O Lord God of Heaven's Armies, hear my prayer.
Listen, O God of Jacob.
O God, look with favor upon my leaders.
Show favor to those You have established.

> *You are the living God.*
> *You are my King and my God.*

A day in Your courts is better than a thousand elsewhere!
I would rather stand at the threshold of the house of my God
   than dwell in the homes of the wicked.
For You are my sun and shield.
You give me grace and glory.
No good thing do You withhold
   from those who do what is right.
O LORD of Heaven's Armies,
   what joy for those who trust in You.

You are my sun and shield.
You give me grace and glory.
You give me good things.

85

Lord, You poured out blessings on me!
You restored my fortunes.
You forgave my guilt—yes, You covered all my sins.
You held back Your fury.
You kept back Your blazing anger.

Now restore me again, O God of my salvation.
Put aside Your anger against me once more.
Will You be angry with me always?
Will You prolong Your wrath to all generations?
Won't You revive me again, so I can rejoice in You?
Show me Your unfailing love, O Lord,
    and grant me Your salvation.

I listen carefully to what You are saying,
    for You speak peace to me.
But let me not return to my foolish ways.
Surely Your salvation is near to those who fear You,
    so my world will be filled with Your glory.

Unfailing love and truth have met together.
Righteousness and peace have kissed!
Truth springs up from the earth,
    and righteousness smiles down from heaven.
Yes, You pour down Your blessings.
My work will be productive.
Righteousness goes as a herald before You,
    preparing the way for Your steps.

> *You speak peace to me.*
> *You pour down Your blessings on me.*

86

Bend down, O LORD, and hear my prayer;
    Answer me, for I need Your help.
Protect me, for I am devoted to You.
Save me, for I serve You and trust You. You are my God.
Be merciful to me, O LORD,
    for I am calling on You constantly.
Give me happiness, O LORD, for I give myself to You.
O LORD, You are so good, so ready to forgive,
    so full of unfailing love for all who ask for Your help.
Listen closely to my prayer, O LORD; Hear my urgent cry.
I will call to You whenever I'm in trouble,
    and You will answer me.

No pagan god is like You, O LORD.
None can do what You do!
All the nations You made will come
    and bow before You, LORD;
    They will praise Your holy name.
For You are great and perform wonderful deeds.
You alone are God.
Teach me Your ways, O LORD,
    that I may live according to Your truth!
Grant me purity of heart, so that I may honor You.
With all my heart I will praise You, O LORD my God.

> *You are my God.*
> *You are so good.*
> *You are so ready to forgive.*
> *You are great and perform wonderful deeds.*
> *You alone are God.*

I will give glory to Your name forever,
    for Your love for me is very great.
You have rescued me from the depths of death.
O God, arrogant men oppose me;
    At times, I feel like they want to kill me.
You mean nothing to them.

But You, O Lord, are a God of compassion and mercy,
    slow to get angry
    and filled with unfailing love and faithfulness.
Look down and have mercy on me.
Give Your strength to me, Your servant;
    Save me, because I serve you just as my mother did.
Send me a sign of Your favor.
Then those who hate me will be put to shame,
    because You, O Lord, have helped and comforted me.

Your love for me is very great.
You have rescued me.
You are a God of compassion and mercy.
You are slow to get angry.
You are filled with unfailing love and faithfulness.

87

On the holy mountain stands the city You founded.
You love the city of Jerusalem
    more than any other city in Israel.
And what glorious things are said of her—Your city.

You will count Egypt and Babylon
    among those who know You—
    also Philistia and Tyre, and even distant Ethiopia.
They have all become citizens of Jerusalem!
Regarding Jerusalem it will be said,
    "Everyone enjoys the rights of citizenship there."
And You will personally bless this city.
When You register the nations, You will say,
    "They have all become citizens of Jerusalem."

The people will play flutes and sing,
    "All my springs of joy are in You."

You love Jerusalem.
You are the source of all joy.

88

Lord, You are the God of my salvation.
I cry to You by day. I come to You at night.
Hear my prayer. Listen to my cry.
For my life is full of troubles, and death draws near.
I am as good as dead, like a strong man with no strength left.
Forsaken among the dead, like a corpse in a grave.
I feel forgotten, cut off from Your care.
You have thrown me into the lowest pit,
    in dark places, in the depths.
Your wrath has rested upon me,
    with wave after wave You have engulfed me.

You have driven my friends away
    by making me repulsive to them.
I am in a trap with no way of escape.
My eyes are blinded by my tears.
Each day I beg for Your help, O Lord;
    I lift my hands to You for mercy.
Are Your wonderful deeds of any use to the dead?
Do the dead rise up and praise You?

Can those in the grave declare Your unfailing love?
Can they proclaim Your faithfulness
    in the place of destruction?
Can the darkness speak of Your wonderful deeds?
Can anyone in the land of forgetfulness
    talk about Your righteousness?
O Lord, I cry out to You.
I will keep on pleading day by day.

You are the God of my salvation.

O LORD, why does it feel like You are rejecting me?
Why does it seem as though
    You have turned Your face from me?

I feel like I have been sick and close to death since my youth.
I stand helpless and desperate before Your terrors.
Your fierce anger has overwhelmed me.
Your terrors have paralyzed me.
They swirl around me like floodwaters all day long.
They have engulfed me completely.

I feel like You have taken away my companions
    and loved ones and made darkness my closest friend.

You are the God of my salvation.

89

I will sing of Your unfailing love forever!
Young and old will hear of Your faithfulness.
Your unfailing love will last forever.
Your faithfulness is as enduring as the heavens.
You have said:

> "I have made a covenant with David, My chosen servant.
> I have sworn this oath to him:
> > 'I will establish your descendants as kings forever;
> > They will sit on your throne from now until eternity.'"

All heaven will praise Your great wonders, LORD;
> Myriads of angels will praise You for Your faithfulness.
For who in all of heaven can compare with You?
What mightiest angel is anything like You, LORD?
The highest angelic powers stand in awe of You.
You are far more awesome
> than all who surround Your throne.

O LORD God of Heaven's Armies!
Where is there anyone as mighty as You, O LORD?
You are entirely faithful.
You rule the oceans.
You subdue their storm-tossed waves.
You crushed the great sea monster.
You scattered Your enemies with Your mighty arm.

Your unfailing love will last forever.
You are entirely faithful.

The heavens are Yours, and the earth is Yours;
Everything in the world is Yours—You created it all.
You created north and south.
Mount Tabor and Mount Hermon praise Your name.
Powerful is Your arm!
Strong is Your hand!
Your right hand is lifted high in glorious strength.

Righteousness and justice are the foundation of Your throne.
Lovingkindness and truth go before You.
Happy are those who hear the joyful call to worship,
for they will walk in the light of Your presence, LORD.
They rejoice all day long in Your wonderful reputation.
They exult in Your righteousness.
You are their glorious strength.
It pleases You to make me strong.
Yes, my protection comes from You, LORD,
and You, the Holy One of Israel, have given me my King.

Long ago You spoke in a vision
to Your faithful people, saying:

"I have raised up a warrior. I have selected him
from the common people to be king.
I have found My servant David.
I have anointed him with My holy oil.
I will steady him with My hand;
With My powerful arm I will make him strong.
His enemies will not defeat him,
nor will the wicked overpower him.
I will beat down his adversaries before him
and destroy those who hate him.

You created everything.
You make me strong.
You protect me.

My faithfulness and unfailing love will be with him,
    and by My authority he will grow in power.
I will extend his rule over the sea,
    his dominion over the rivers.
And he will call out to Me, 'You are my Father,
    my God, and the Rock of my salvation.'
I will make him, My firstborn son,
    the mightiest king on earth.
I will love him and be kind to him forever;
    My covenant with him will never end.
I will preserve an heir for him;
    His throne will be as endless as the days of heaven.

But if his descendants forsake My instructions
    and fail to obey My regulations,
    if they do not obey My decrees
    and fail to keep My commands,
    then I will punish their sin with the rod
    and their disobedience with beating.
But I will never stop loving him
    nor fail to keep My promise to him.
No, I will not break My covenant;
    I will not take back a single word I said.
I have sworn an oath to David,
    and in My holiness I cannot lie.
His dynasty will go on forever;
    His kingdom will endure as the sun.
It will be as eternal as the moon,
    My faithful witness in the sky."

You cannot lie.

But then You rejected him and cast him off.
You were angry with Your anointed king.
You renounced Your covenant with him;
    You threw his crown in the dust.
You broke down the walls protecting him
    and ruined every fort defending him.
Everyone who came along robbed him,
    and he became a joke to his neighbors.
You strengthened his enemies and made them all rejoice.
You made his sword useless and refused to help him in battle.
You ended his splendor and overturned his throne.
You made him old before his time
    and publicly disgraced him.

O Lord, when I feel abandoned by You, I ask:
    "How long will this go on?
    Will You hide Yourself forever?
    How long will Your anger burn like fire?"
Remember how short my life is,
    How empty and futile is this human existence!
No one can live forever; All will die.
No one can escape the power of the grave.

Lord, where is Your unfailing love?
You promised it to David with a faithful pledge.
Consider, Lord, how Your servants are disgraced!
I carry in my heart the insults of so many people.
Your enemies have mocked me, O Lord;
    And they mock Your anointed.
I will praise You forever, Lord.
Amen and amen!

You promise Your unfailing love.

90

Lord, through all the generations You have been man's home!
Before the mountains were born,
> before You gave birth to the earth and the world,
> from beginning to end, You are God.

You turn people back to dust, saying,
> "Return to dust, you mortals!"
For You, a thousand years are as a passing day,
> as brief as a few night hours.
You sweep people away like dreams that disappear.
They are like grass that springs up in the morning.
In the morning it blooms and flourishes,
> but by evening it is dry and withered.

I wither beneath Your anger;
> I am overwhelmed by Your fury.
You spread out my sins before You—
> my secret sins—and You see them all.
I live my life beneath Your wrath,
> ending my years with a groan.
Seventy years are given to me! Maybe eighty.
But even the best years are filled with pain and trouble;
> Soon they disappear, and I will fly away.
Who can comprehend the power of Your anger?
Your wrath is as awesome as the fear You deserve.
Teach me to realize the brevity of life,
> so that I may grow in wisdom.

You are God.
You see all my secret sins.

152

O Lord, come back to me!
How long will You delay?
Take pity on me, Your servant.

Satisfy me each morning with Your unfailing love,
    so I may sing for joy to the end of my life.
Give me gladness in proportion to my former misery.
Replace the evil years with good.
Let me, Your servant, see You work again;
    Let my children see Your glory.

O Lord, my God, show me Your approval
    and make my efforts successful.
Yes, make my efforts successful!

Your love is unfailing.

91

You tell me that when I abide in Your shelter, Almighty God,
 I will find rest in Your shadow.
This I declare about You, LORD:
 You alone are my refuge, my place of safety;
 You are my God, and I trust You.
For You will rescue me from every trap
 and protect me from deadly disease.
You will cover me with Your feathers.
You will shelter me with Your wings.
Your faithful promises are my armor and protection.

I will not be afraid of the terrors of the night,
 nor the arrow that flies in the day.
I will not dread the disease that stalks in darkness,
 nor the disaster that strikes at midday.
Though a thousand fall at my side,
 though ten thousand are dying around me,
 I know that these evils will not touch me.
I will just open my eyes
 and see how the wicked are punished.
If I make You my refuge, if I make You my shelter,
 no evil will conquer me;
 No plague will come near my home.

For You will give Your angels charge concerning me,
 to guard me in all my ways.
They will bear me up in their hands,
 that I do not strike my foot against a stone.
I will tread upon the lion and cobra;
 The young lion and the serpent I will trample down.

You alone are my refuge, my place of safety.
You hear me when I call.

You say that, because I love You, You will rescue me
    and protect me, because I trust in Your name.
You promise that, when I call on You, You will answer me
    and be with me in trouble and will rescue and honor me.
You will reward me with a long life
    and give me Your salvation.

You are my salvation.

92

It is good to give thanks to You, Lord,
    to sing praises to You, the Most High.
It is good to proclaim Your unfailing love in the morning,
    Your faithfulness in the evening,
    accompanied by a ten-stringed instrument,
    a harp, and the melody of a lyre.

You thrill me, Lord, with all You have done for me!
I sing for joy because of what You have done.
O Lord, what great works You do!
And how deep are Your thoughts.
A senseless man has no knowledge,
    and only a fool would not understand this:
That when the wicked sprouted up like grass
    and evildoers flourished,
    it was only that they might be destroyed forevermore.

But You, O Lord, will be exalted forever.
Your enemies, Lord, will surely perish;
    All evildoers will be scattered.
But You have made me as strong as a wild ox.
You have anointed me with the finest oil.
My eyes have seen the downfall of my enemies;
    My ears have heard the defeat of my wicked opponents.

Your love is unfailing.
You are forever faithful.
You do great works.

You assure me that, as a righteous man,
    I will flourish like the palm tree.
I will grow strong like a cedar in Lebanon.
Planted in Your house, I will flourish in Your courts.
Even in old age, I will still produce fruit
    and remain vital and green.
I will declare, "The LORD is just! He is my rock!
    There is no evil in Him!"

You are just.
You are my rock.

93

You, LORD, are king! You are robed in majesty.
Indeed, You are robed in majesty and armed with strength.
The world stands firm and cannot be shaken.

Your throne, O LORD, is established from of old;
    You are from everlasting.
The floods have risen up, O LORD.
The floods have roared like thunder;
    The floods have lifted their pounding waves.
But mightier than the violent raging of the seas,
    mightier than the breakers on the shore—
    You are mightier than these!
Your royal laws cannot be changed.
Your reign, O LORD, is holy forever and ever.

You are King.
You are robed in majesty.
You are eternal.
You are mightier than the violent raging of the seas.
You are mightier than the breakers on the shore.
You are holy.

94

O LORD, God of vengeance,
    O God of vengeance, let Your glorious justice shine forth!
Rise up, O Judge of the earth.
Give the proud what they deserve.
How long, O LORD?
How long will the wicked be allowed to gloat?
How long will they speak with arrogance?
How long will these evil people boast?
They crush Your people, LORD,
    hurting those You claim as Your own.
They kill widows and foreigners and murder orphans.
"The LORD isn't looking," they say,
    "and besides, the God of Israel doesn't care."

I want to say, "Think again, you fools!
    When will you finally catch on?
    Is He deaf—the One who made your ears?
    Is He blind—the One who formed your eyes?
    He punishes the nations—won't He also punish you?
    He knows everything—
        doesn't He also know what you are doing?"

You know people's thoughts; You know they are worthless!
Joyful are those You discipline, LORD,
    those You teach with Your instructions.
You give them relief from troubled times
    until a pit is dug to capture the wicked.
You will not reject Your people;
    You will not abandon Your special possession.
Judgment will again be founded on justice,
    and those with virtuous hearts will pursue it.

> *You know people's thoughts.*
> *You will not abandon Your people.*

Who will protect me from the wicked?
Who will stand up for me against evildoers?
Unless You had helped me,
    I would soon have settled in the silence of the grave.
I cried out, "I am slipping!"
But Your unfailing love, O LORD, supported me.
When doubts filled my mind,
    Your comfort gave me renewed hope and cheer.
Can unjust leaders claim that You are on their side—
    leaders whose decrees permit injustice?

They gang up against the righteous
    and condemn the innocent to death.
But You are my fortress;
    You are the mighty rock where I hide.
You will turn the sins of evil people back on them.
You will destroy them for their sins.
You, LORD, my God, will destroy them.

You are my fortress.
You are the mighty rock.
You will destroy evil people.

95

I will sing for joy to You, LORD.
I will shout joyfully to the Rock of my salvation.
I will come before Your presence with thanksgiving.
I will shout joyfully to You with psalms.
For You, LORD, are a great God
    and a great King above all gods.
In Your hand are the depths of the earth,
    and the peaks of the mountains are Yours also.
The sea is Yours, for it was You who made it,
    and Your hands formed the dry land.
I will worship and bow down.
I will kneel before You, LORD, my Maker.
For You are my God, and I am Yours.
You watch over me, as part of the flock under Your care.
Enable me to hear Your voice, LORD.
You have commanded me to not harden my heart,
    as Israel did at Meribah,
    as they did at Massah in the wilderness,
    when my forefathers tested You and tried You,
    though they had seen Your work.
For forty years You were angry with them
    and said that they were a people
    whose hearts turn away from You.
They refused to do what You told them.
Therefore, in Your anger, You swore that
    they would never enter Your place of rest.
Please let that never be my fate, LORD.

> *You are a great God.*
> *You are a great King, above all gods.*
> *You made the sea and the land.*
> *You made me and watch over me.*
> *You speak to me.*
> *You welcome me into Your place of rest.*

96

I will sing a new song to You, LORD!
May the whole earth sing to You!
I will sing to You, LORD and praise Your name.
Each day I will proclaim the good news that You save.
I will publish Your glorious deeds among the nations.
I will tell everyone about the amazing things You do.
Great are You LORD! You are most worthy of praise!
You are to be feared above all gods.
The gods of other nations are mere idols,
    but You made the heavens!
Honor and majesty surround You;
    Strength and beauty fill Your sanctuary.

The nations of the world will recognize You, LORD;
    They will recognize that You are glorious and strong.
I will give You the glory You deserve.
I will bring my offering and come into Your courts.
I will worship You, LORD, in all Your holy splendor.
May all the earth tremble before You.
I will tell all the nations that You reign,
    that the world stands firm and cannot be shaken,
    and that You will judge all peoples fairly.

You save.
You are great.
You are worthy of praise.
You are to be feared.
You made the heavens.
You deserve all glory.
You reign.
You will judge everyone fairly.

May the heavens be glad, and the earth rejoice!
May the sea and everything in it shout Your praise!
May the fields and their crops burst out with joy!
May the trees of the forest sing for joy before You,
    for You are coming!
You are coming to judge the earth.
You will judge the world with justice
    and the nations with Your truth.

You are coming to judge the earth.

97

You reign, may the earth be glad;
  May the distant shores rejoice.
Clouds and thick darkness surround You;
  Righteousness and justice
  are the foundation of Your throne.
Fire goes before You and consumes Your foes on every side.
Your lightning lights up the world;
  The earth sees and trembles.
The mountains melt like wax before You,
  before You, the LORD of all the earth.
The heavens proclaim Your righteousness,
  and all peoples see Your glory.

Those who worship idols are disgraced—
  all who brag about their worthless gods—
  for every god must bow to You.
Jerusalem has heard and rejoiced,
  and all the towns of Judah are glad
  because of Your justice, O LORD!
For You, O LORD, are supreme over all the earth;
  You are exalted far above all gods.
I love You LORD. Teach me to hate evil.
You protect the lives of Your faithful followers
  and rescue them from the power of the wicked.
Light shines on the godly,
  and joy on those whose hearts are right.
May all who are godly rejoice in You, LORD,
  and praise Your holy name!

You reign.
You are supreme over all the earth.
You protect the lives of Your faithful followers.

98

I will sing a new song to You, Lord,
    for You have done wonderful things.
Your right hand and Your holy arm
    have gained the victory for You.
You have made known Your salvation.
You have revealed Your righteousness to every nation.
You have remembered Your promise to love
    and be faithful to Israel.
The ends of the earth have seen Your salvation.

May the whole earth shout joyfully to You, Lord
    and break out in praise and sing for joy
    and sing Your praise with the harp,
    with the harp and the sound of melody,
    and with trumpets and the sound of the horn,
    making a joyful symphony before You, Lord, my King!

May the sea and everything in it shout Your praise!
May the earth and all living things join in.
May the rivers clap their hands in glee!
May the hills sing out their songs of joy
    before You, Lord,
    for You are coming to judge the earth.
You will judge the world with justice,
    and the nations with fairness.

You have done wonderful things.
You have made known Your salvation.
You have revealed Your righteousness to every nation.
You are coming to judge the world with justice and fairness.

99

You, LORD, are king!
Make the nations tremble!
You sit on Your throne between the cherubim.
Make the whole earth quake!
You, LORD, sit in majesty in Jerusalem,
    exalted above all the nations.
Let them praise Your great and awesome name.
Your name is holy!

Mighty King, lover of justice,
    You have established fairness.
You have acted with justice
    and righteousness throughout Israel.
I will exalt You, LORD, my God!
I will bow low before Your feet, for You are holy!
Moses and Aaron were among Your priests.
Samuel also called on Your name.

They cried to You, LORD, for help,
    and You answered them.
You spoke to Israel from the pillar of cloud,
    and they followed the laws and decrees You gave them.
O LORD, my God, You answered them.
You were a forgiving God to them,
    but You punished them when they went wrong.

I will exalt You, LORD, my God!
    and worship at Your holy mountain in Jerusalem,
    for You, LORD, my God, are holy!

You are my king.
Your name is holy.
You are holy.

100

I will shout joyfully to You, LORD.
I will serve You with gladness.

I will come before You with joyful singing.
I know that You Yourself are God.

It is You who has made me, and not me myself.
I am Yours, a sheep of Your pasture.

I will enter Your gates with thanksgiving
    and Your courts with praise.

I will give thanks to You and bless Your name.
For You are good.

Your lovingkindness is everlasting
    and Your faithfulness is to all generations.

You are God.
You made me.
You are good.
Your love and Your faithfulness endure forever.

101

I will sing of Your love and justice, LORD.
I will praise You with songs.
I will be careful to live a blameless life.

When will You come to help me?
I will lead a life of integrity in my own home.
I will set no worthless thing before my eyes.
I hate the work of those who fall away.
It shall not fasten its grip on me.
A perverse heart shall depart from me;
    I will know no evil.
I will not tolerate people who slander their neighbors.
I will not endure conceit and pride.

I will search for faithful people to be my companions.
Only those who are above reproach will minister to me.
I will not allow deceivers to serve in my house,
    and liars will not stay in my presence.

LORD, give me a heart that hates wickedness as David did,
    as he each day sought to destroy all the wicked of the land,
    and to cut them off from Your city.

You deserve my praise and my full devotion.

102

LORD, hear my prayer! Listen to my plea!
Don't turn away from me in my time of distress.
Bend down to listen,
    and answer me quickly when I call to You.
For my days disappear like smoke,
    and my bones burn like red-hot coals.
My heart is sick, withered like grass,
    and I have lost my appetite.
Because of my groaning, I am reduced to skin and bones.
I am like an owl in the desert,
    like a little owl in a far-off wilderness.
I lie awake, lonely as a solitary bird on the roof.
My enemies taunt me day after day. They mock and curse me.
I feel like David, who ate ashes for food
    and whose tears ran down into his drink
    because of Your anger and wrath.
I feel like You have picked me up and thrown me out.
My life passes as swiftly as the evening shadows.
I am withering away like grass.

But You, O LORD, will sit on Your throne forever.
Your fame will endure to every generation.
You will arise and have mercy on Jerusalem—
    for now is the time to be gracious to her,
    now is the time You promised to help.
For Your people love every stone in her walls
    and cherish even the dust in her streets.
Then the nations will tremble before You, LORD.
The kings of the earth will tremble before Your glory.

You will sit on Your throne forever.

For You will rebuild Jerusalem.
You will appear in Your glory.
You will listen to the prayers of the destitute.
You will not reject their pleas.

Let this be recorded for future generations,
    so that a people not yet born will praise You, LORD.
For You looked down from Your heavenly sanctuary.
You looked down to earth from heaven
    to hear the groans of the prisoners,
    to release those condemned to die.
And so Your fame will be celebrated in Zion,
    Your praises in Jerusalem,
    when multitudes gather together
    and kingdoms come to worship You, LORD.

You broke my strength in midlife, cutting short my days.
But I cried to You:

    O my God, who lives forever,
        don't take my life while I am so young!
    Long ago You laid the foundation of the earth
        and made the heavens with Your hands.
    They will perish, but You remain forever;
        They will wear out like old clothing.
    You will change them like a garment and discard them.
    But You are always the same; You will live forever.
    The children of Your people will live in security.
    Their children's children will thrive in Your presence.

You will appear in Your glory.
You live forever.
You laid the foundation of the earth.

103

Let all that I am praise You, LORD;
  And all that is within me, I will praise Your holy name.
Let all that I am praise You, LORD;
  And may I never forget all that You have done
  and do for me.
You forgive all my sins and heal all my diseases.
You redeem me from death
  and crown me with love and compassion.
You fill my life with good things,
  so that my youth is renewed like the eagle.

You perform righteous deeds
  and judgments for all who are oppressed.
You made known Your ways to Moses,
  Your acts to the sons of Israel.
You are compassionate and gracious,
  Slow to anger and abounding in lovingkindness.
You will not always strive with me,
  nor will You keep Your anger forever.
You have not dealt with me according to my sins,
  nor rewarded me according to my iniquities.
For as high as the heavens are above the earth,
  so great is Your lovingkindness
  toward those who fear You.
As far as the east is from the west,
  so far have You removed my transgressions from me.

> *You forgive all my sins.*
> *You fill my life with good things.*
> *You are compassionate and gracious.*
> *You are slow to anger.*
> *You remove my transgressions from me.*

Just as a father has compassion on his children,
  so You have compassion on those who fear You.
For You know how weak I am;
  You remember I am only dust.
As for me, my days are like grass;
  Like a wildflower, I bloom and then die.
The wind blows, and I am gone,
  as though I had never been here.
But Your love remains forever with those who fear You.
Your salvation extends to the children's children
  of those who keep Your covenant,
  of those who obey Your commandments.

You have made the heavens Your throne;
  And, from there, You rule over everything.
May all of Your angels praise You, LORD;
  Those mighty in strength,
  who perform Your word, obeying the voice of Your word!
May all of Your armies of angels praise You, LORD;
  Those who serve You and do Your will.
May all that You have created, praise You, LORD,
  everything in Your kingdom.
Let all that I am praise You, LORD.

You rule over everything.

104

Let all that I am praise You, LORD.
O LORD my God, how great You are!
You are robed with honor and majesty.
You are dressed in a robe of light.
You stretch out the starry curtain of the heavens.
You lay out the rafters of Your home in the rain clouds.
You make the clouds Your chariot.
You ride upon the wings of the wind.
The winds are Your messengers;
    Flames of fire are Your servants.

You placed the world on its foundation
    so it would never be moved.
You clothed the earth with floods of water,
    water that covered even the mountains.
At Your command, the water fled;
    At the sound of Your thunder, it hurried away.
Mountains rose and valleys sank to the levels You decreed.
Then You set a firm boundary for the seas,
    so they would never again cover the earth.

You make springs pour water into the ravines,
    so streams gush down from the mountains.
They provide water for all the animals,
    and the wild donkeys quench their thirst.
The birds nest beside the streams
    and sing among the branches of the trees.

You are great.
You created everything.

You send rain on the mountains from Your heavenly home,
and You fill the earth with the fruit of Your labor.
You cause grass to grow for the livestock
and plants for people to use.
You allow them to produce food from the earth—
wine to make them glad,
olive oil to soothe their skin,
and bread to give them strength.
Your trees are well cared for—
the cedars of Lebanon that You planted.

There, the birds make their nests,
and the storks make their homes in the cypresses.
High in the mountains live the wild goats,
and the rocks form a refuge for the hyraxes.
You made the moon to mark the seasons,
and the sun knows when to set.
You send the darkness, and it becomes night,
when all the forest animals prowl about.
Then the young lions roar for their prey,
stalking the food You provided.
At dawn they slink back into their dens to rest.
Then people go off to their work,
where they labor until evening.

O Lord, what a variety of things You have made!
In wisdom, You have made them all.
The earth is full of Your creatures.
Here is the ocean, vast and wide,
teeming with life of every kind, both large and small.

You maintain everything.

I see the ships sailing along, and Leviathan,
  which You made to play in the sea.
They all depend on You to give them food as they need it.
When You supply it, they gather it.
You open Your hand to feed them,
  and they are richly satisfied.
But if You turn away from them, they panic.
When You take away their breath,
  they die and turn again to dust.
When You give them Your breath, life is created,
  and You renew the face of the earth.

May Your glory continue forever!
You take pleasure in all You have made!
The earth trembles at Your glance;
  The mountains smoke at Your touch.
I will sing to You, LORD, as long as I live.
I will praise You, my God, to my last breath!
May all my thoughts be pleasing to You,
  for I rejoice in You, LORD.
Let all sinners vanish from the face of the earth;
  Let the wicked disappear forever.
Let all that I am praise You, LORD.
I Praise You, LORD!

You take pleasure in all You have made.

105

I give thanks to You, LORD, and proclaim Your greatness.
I will do my part to let the whole world know
    what You have done.
I will sing to You; Yes, sing Your praises.
I will tell everyone about Your wonderful deeds.
I will exult in Your holy name
    and rejoice as I worship You, LORD.
I will search for You, LORD, and for Your strength.
I will continually seek You.
As You commanded the children of Your servant Abraham,
    (the descendants of Jacob, Your chosen ones),
      I will remember the wonders You have performed,
      Your miracles, and the rulings You have given.
You are the LORD my God.
Your justice is seen throughout the land.
You always stand by Your covenant—
    the commitment You made to a thousand generations.
This is the covenant You made with Abraham
    and the oath You swore to Isaac.
You confirmed it to Jacob as a decree,
    and to the people of Israel as a never-ending covenant:
    "I will give you the land of Canaan
    as your special possession."
You said this when they were few in number,
    a tiny group of strangers in Canaan.
They wandered from nation to nation,
    from one kingdom to another.
Yet You did not let anyone oppress them.
You warned kings on their behalf:
    "Do not touch My chosen people,
    and do not hurt My prophets."

> *You are great.*
> *You stand by Your covenant.*

You called for a famine on the land of Canaan,
cutting off its food supply.
Then You sent someone to Egypt ahead of them—
Joseph, who was sold as a slave.
They bruised his feet with fetters
and placed his neck in an iron collar.
Until the time came to fulfill his dreams,
You tested Joseph's character.
Then Pharaoh sent for him and set him free;
The ruler of the nation opened his prison door.
Joseph was put in charge of all the king's household;
He became ruler over all the king's possessions.
He could instruct the king's aides as he pleased
and teach the king's advisers.
Then Israel arrived in Egypt;
Jacob lived as a foreigner in the land of Ham.
And You multiplied the people of Israel
until they became too mighty for their enemies.

Then You turned the Egyptians against the Israelites,
and they plotted against Your servants.
But You sent Your servant Moses, along with Aaron,
whom You had chosen.
They performed miraculous signs among the Egyptians,
and wonders in the land of Ham.
You blanketed Egypt in darkness,
for they had defied Your commands to let Your people go.
You turned their water into blood, poisoning all the fish.
Then frogs overran the land
and even invaded the king's bedrooms.
When You spoke, flies descended on the Egyptians,
and gnats swarmed across Egypt.
You sent them hail instead of rain,
and lightning flashed over the land.

You orchestrate everything.

You ruined their grapevines and fig trees
and shattered all the trees.
You spoke, and hordes of locusts came—
young locusts beyond number.
They ate up everything green in the land,
destroying all the crops in their fields.
Then You killed the oldest son in each Egyptian home,
the pride and joy of each family.

You brought Your people out of Egypt,
loaded with silver and gold;
And not one among the tribes of Israel even stumbled.
Egypt was glad when they were gone,
for they feared them greatly.
You spread a cloud above them as a covering
and gave them a great fire to light the darkness.
They asked for meat, and You sent them quail.
You satisfied their hunger with manna—bread from heaven.
You split open a rock, and water gushed out
to form a river through the dry wasteland.
For You remembered Your sacred promise
to Your servant Abraham.
So You brought Your people out of Egypt with joy,
Your chosen ones with rejoicing.
You gave Your people the lands of pagan nations,
and they harvested crops that others had planted.
All this happened so they would follow Your decrees
and obey Your instructions.
I praise You, LORD!

You brought Your people out of Egypt.
You satisfied their hunger.

106

I praise You, Lord!
I give thanks to You, for You are good!
Your faithful love endures forever.
Who can list Your glorious miracles?
Who can ever praise You enough?
You tell me that there is joy for me if I deal justly with others
    and always do what is right.

Remember me, Lord, when You show favor to Your people;
    Come near and rescue me.
Let me share in the prosperity of Your chosen ones.
Let me rejoice in the joy of Your people.
Let me praise You with those who are Your heritage.

Like all those before me, I have sinned.
I have done wrong! I have acted wickedly!
Your people in Egypt were not impressed
    by Your miraculous deeds.
They soon forgot Your many acts of kindness to them.
Instead, they rebelled against You at the Red Sea.
Even so, You saved them—to defend the honor of Your name
    and to demonstrate Your mighty power.
You commanded the Red Sea to dry up.
You led Israel across the sea as if it were a desert.
So You rescued them from their enemies
    and redeemed them from their foes.
Then the water returned and covered their enemies;
    Not one of them survived.
Then Your people believed Your promises.
Then they sang Your praise.

You are good.

Yet how quickly they forgot what You had done!
They wouldn't wait for Your counsel!
In the wilderness their desires ran wild,
    testing Your patience in that dry wasteland.
So You gave them what they asked for,
    but You sent a plague along with it.

The people in the camp were jealous of Moses
    and envious of Aaron, Your holy priest.
Because of this, the earth opened up;
    It swallowed Dathan and buried Abiram
    and the other rebels.
Fire fell upon their followers; A flame consumed the wicked.

The people made a calf at Mount Sinai;
    They bowed before an image made of gold.
They traded You, their glorious God,
    for a statue of a grass-eating bull.
They forgot You, their savior,
    who had done such great things in Egypt—
    such wonderful things in the land of Ham,
    such awesome deeds at the Red Sea.
So You declared You would destroy them.
But Moses, Your chosen one,
    stepped between You and the people.
He begged You to turn from Your anger
    and not destroy them.
The people refused to enter the pleasant land,
    for they wouldn't believe Your promise to care for them.
Instead, they grumbled in their tents and refused to obey You.
Therefore, You solemnly swore
    that You would kill them in the wilderness,
    that You would scatter their descendants
    among the nations, exiling them to distant lands.

You are so patient.

Then they joined in the worship of Baal at Peor;
    They even ate sacrifices offered to the dead!
They angered You with all these things,
    so a plague broke out among them.
But Phinehas had the courage to intervene,
    and the plague was stopped.
So he has been regarded as a righteous man
    ever since that time.
At Meribah, too, they angered You, LORD,
    causing Moses serious trouble.
They made Moses angry, and he spoke foolishly.

Israel failed to destroy the nations in the land,
    as You had commanded them.
Instead, they mingled among the pagans
    and adopted their evil customs.
They worshiped their idols, which led to their downfall.
They even sacrificed their sons
    and their daughters to the demons.
They shed innocent blood,
    the blood of their sons and daughters.
By sacrificing them to the idols of Canaan
    they polluted the land with murder.
They defiled themselves by their evil deeds,
    and their love of idols was adultery in Your sight.

That is why Your anger burned against Your people,
    and You abhorred Your own special possession.
You handed them over to pagan nations,
    and they were ruled by those who hated them.
Their enemies crushed them
    and brought them under their cruel power.

You get angry when I turn from You.

Again and again You rescued them,
　　but they chose to rebel against You,
　　and they were finally destroyed by their sin.
Even so, You pitied them in their distress
　　and listened to their cries.
You remembered Your covenant with them
　　and relented because of Your unfailing love.
You even caused their captors to treat them with kindness.

Save me, O LORD my God!
Gather me back from among the nations,
　　so I can thank Your holy name and rejoice and praise You.
I praise You, LORD, God of Israel,
　　who lives from everlasting to everlasting!
Let all the people say, "Amen!"
I praise You, LORD!

Your love is unfailing.

107

I give thanks to You, LORD, for You are good!
Your faithful love endures forever.
You have redeemed me. So, I will speak out!
I will tell others that You have redeemed me
    from my enemies.
For You have gathered the exiles from many lands,
    from east and west, from north and south.
Some wandered in the wilderness, lost and homeless.
Hungry and thirsty, they nearly died.
"LORD, help!" they cried in their trouble,
    and You rescued them from their distress.
You led them straight to safety,
    to a city where they could live.
I will praise You, LORD, for Your great love
    and for the wonderful things You have done.
For You satisfy the thirsty soul
    and fill the hungry with good things.

Some sat in darkness and deepest gloom,
    imprisoned in iron chains of misery.
They rebelled against Your words, scorning Your counsel.
That is why You broke them with hard labor;
    They fell, and no one was there to help them.
"LORD, help!" they cried in their trouble,
    and You saved them from their distress.
You led them from the darkness and deepest gloom;
    You snapped their chains.
I will praise You, LORD, for Your great love
    and for the wonderful things You have done.
For You broke down their prison gates of bronze;
    You cut apart their bars of iron.

You are good.
You satisfy the thirsty soul.

Some were fools; They rebelled and suffered for their sins.
They couldn't stand the thought of food,
    and they were knocking on death's door.
"LORD, help!" they cried in their trouble,
    and You saved them from their distress.
You sent out Your word and healed them,
    and saved them from their destruction.
I will praise You, LORD, for Your great love
    and for the wonderful things You have done.
I will offer sacrifices of thanksgiving
    and sing joyfully about Your glorious acts.

Some went off to sea in ships,
    doing business on the great waters.
They, too, observed Your power in action,
    Your impressive works on the deepest seas.
You spoke, and the winds rose, stirring up the waves.
Their ships were tossed to the heavens
    and plunged again to the depths;
    The sailors cringed in terror.
They reeled and staggered like drunkards
    and were at their wits' end.
"LORD, help!" they cried in their trouble,
    and You saved them from their distress.
You calmed the storm to a whisper and stilled the waves.
What a blessing was that stillness
    as You brought them safely into harbor!
I will praise You, LORD, for Your great love
    and for the wonderful things You have done.
I will exalt You publicly before the congregation
    and before the leaders of the nation.

You are so powerful.
Your love is great.
You have done wonderful things.

You change rivers into deserts
    and springs of water into dry, thirsty land.
You turn the fruitful land into salty wastelands,
    because of the wickedness of those who live there.
But You also turn deserts into pools of water,
    the dry land into springs of water.
You bring the hungry to settle there and to build their cities.
They sow their fields, plant their vineyards,
    and harvest their bumper crops.
How You bless them!
They raise large families there,
    and their herds of livestock increase.

When they decrease in number and become impoverished
    through oppression, trouble, and sorrow,
    You pour contempt on their princes,
    causing them to wander in trackless wastelands.
But You rescue the poor from trouble
    and increase their families like flocks of sheep.
The godly will see these things and be glad,
    while the wicked are struck silent.
LORD, give me wisdom, to take all this to heart
    and to consider Your faithful love.

You rescue the poor from trouble.

108

My heart is steadfast, O God.
I will sing. I will sing praises, even with my soul.
I will awaken the dawn with my song!
I will give thanks to You, O LORD, among the peoples,
    and I will sing praises to You among the nations.
For Your lovingkindness is great above the heavens,
    and Your truth reaches to the skies.
Be exalted, O God, above the heavens,
    and Your glory above all the earth.
Rescue me, Your beloved, LORD.
Answer me and save me with Your right hand.

You promised, in Your holiness,
    that You would divide up Shechem with joy
    and measure out the valley of Succoth.
You claimed Gilead and Manasseh as Yours.
You called Ephraim Your helmet
    and said that it would produce Your warriors,
You called Judah Your scepter
    and said that it would produce Your kings.
But Moab, You called Your washbowl
    and said that it would become Your servant,
You also said that You would wipe Your feet on Edom
    and shout in triumph over Philistia.

Your lovingkindness is great above the heavens.
Your truth reaches to the skies.

Will You bring me, Lord,
    through my tough battles and into safety?
Will You bring me victory over my enemies?
O God, it sure feels like You have rejected me.
Won't You go with me into battle?
Oh, Lord, give me help against the adversary,
    for all human help is useless.
With Your help, God, I know I will do mighty things,
    for You will trample down my adversaries.

You will trample down my adversaries.

109

O God, whom I praise, don't be silent!
Should the wicked slander me and tell lies about me
 and surround me with hateful words
 and fight against me for no reason?
In return for my love, if they accuse me,
 though I devote myself to prayer;
 If they repay evil for good and hatred for my love;
 If they say:

 "Get an evil person to turn against her.
 Send an accuser to bring her to trial.
 When her case comes up for judgment,
  let her be pronounced guilty.
 Count her prayers as sins. Let her years be few;
  Let someone else take her position.
 May her children become motherless, and her husband a widower.
 May her children wander as beggars
  and be driven from their ruined homes.
 May creditors seize her entire estate,
  and strangers take all she has earned.
 Let no one be kind to her;
  Let no one pity her motherless children.
 May all her offspring die.
 May her family name be blotted out in the next generation.
 May the LORD never forget the sins of her fathers.
 May her mother's sins never be erased from the record.
 May the LORD always remember these sins,
  and may her name disappear from human memory.
 For she refused all kindness to others;
  She persecuted the poor and needy,
  and she hounded the brokenhearted to death.
 She loved to curse others; Now You curse her.

> *You are worthy of praise.*

She never blessed others; Now don't You bless her.
Cursing is as natural to her as her clothing,
    or the water she drinks, or the rich food she eats.
Now may her curses return and cling to her like clothing;
    May they be tied around her like a belt."

If You choose to apply these curses to my accusers
    who speak evil of me,
    let such punishment be exactly what is needed
    for them to turn to You.
But deal well with me, O Sovereign LORD,
    for the sake of Your own reputation!
Rescue me because You are so faithful and good.
For I am poor and needy, and my heart is full of pain.
I am fading like a shadow at dusk;
    I am brushed off like a locust.
My knees are weak from fasting, and I am skin and bones.
If I become a joke to people everywhere;
    If when they see me, they shake their heads in scorn.
Help me, O LORD my God!
Save me because of Your unfailing love.
Let them see that this is Your doing,
    that You Yourself have done it, LORD.
Then let them curse me if they like, but You will bless me!
When they attack me, they will be disgraced!
But I, Your servant, will go right on rejoicing!
May my accusers be clothed with disgrace;
    May their humiliation cover them like a cloak.
But I will give repeated thanks to You, LORD,
    praising You to everyone.
For You stand beside the needy,
    ready to save them from those who condemn them.

You are so faithful and good.
You stand beside the needy.
You stand ready to save.

110

GOD, You say to Jesus, my Lord:
"Sit in the place of honor at My right hand
until I humble Your enemies,
making them a footstool under Your feet."
You will extend His scepter from Jerusalem, saying:
"Rule in the midst of Your enemies."

When He goes to war, His people will serve Him willingly.
He will be arrayed in holy garments,
and His strength will be renewed each day
like the morning dew.

GOD, You have sworn and will not break Your vow:
"You are a priest forever in the order of Melchizedek."

He is at Your right hand.
He will strike down many kings when His anger erupts.
He will punish the nations and fill their lands with corpses.
He will shatter heads over the whole earth.
He will be refreshed from brooks along the way.
He will be victorious.

You give dominion to the King.

111

I praise You, LORD!

I will thank You with all my heart
  as I meet with Your godly people.
How amazing are Your deeds, LORD!
All who delight in You should ponder them.
Everything You do reveals Your glory and majesty.
Your righteousness never fails.
You cause me to remember Your wonderful works.
How gracious and merciful are You, my LORD!
You give food to those who fear You;
  You always remember Your covenant.
You have shown Your great power to Your people
  by giving them the lands of other nations.
All You do is just and good,
  and all Your commandments are trustworthy.
They are forever true,
  to be obeyed faithfully and with integrity.
You have paid a full ransom for Your people.
You have guaranteed Your covenant with them forever.
What a holy, awe-inspiring name You have!
Fear of You, LORD, is the foundation of true wisdom.
All who obey Your commandments will grow in wisdom.

I will praise You forever!

> *Your deeds are amazing.*
> *Your righteousness never fails.*
> *You give food to those who fear You.*
> *You always remember Your covenant.*
> *You have paid my ransom in full.*
> *Your name is holy and awe-inspiring.*

112

I praise You, Lord!

Teach me to fear You, Lord,
    and to delight in obeying Your commands.
You tell me that, if I do so:

-    My children will be successful;
-    An entire generation of godly people will be blessed;
-    Wealth and riches will be in my house;
-    My righteousness will endure forever; and
-    Light will arise in the darkness for me.

You tell me that, if I am gracious, merciful, and righteous;
    lend money generously; and conduct my business fairly:

-    It will go well with me;
-    I will not be overcome by evil;
-    I will be long remembered;
-    I will not fear bad news;
-    I will confidently trust You to care for me;
-    I will be confident and fearless
        and be able to face my foes triumphantly;
-    I will share freely and give generously to those in need;
-    My good deeds will be remembered forever; and
-    I will have influence and honor.

The wicked will see this and be infuriated.
They will grind their teeth in anger;
    They will slink away, their hopes thwarted.

You bless those who fear You and walk in Your way.

113

I praise You, LORD!

Yes, I give You praise, as Your servant, LORD.
I praise Your name, LORD!
Blessed be Your name now and forever.
Everywhere—from east to west—
    I praise Your name, LORD.
For You are high above the nations;
    Your glory is higher than the heavens.

Who can be compared with You, LORD, my God,
    You who are enthroned on high?
You stoop to look down
    on heaven and on earth.
You lift the poor from the dust
    and the needy from the garbage dump.
You set them among princes,
    even the princes of Your own people!
You give the childless woman a family,
    making her a happy mother.

I praise You, LORD!

> *You are high above the nations.*
> *Your glory is higher than the heavens.*
> *You are beyond comparison.*
> *You are enthroned on high.*
> *You care for the poor.*

114

When the Israelites escaped from Egypt—
    when the family of Jacob left that foreign land—
    the land of Judah became Your sanctuary,
    and Israel became Your kingdom.

The Red Sea saw them coming and fled;
    The water of the Jordan River turned away.
The mountains skipped like rams, the hills like lambs!
Had I been there, I likely would have mocked:

      "What's wrong, Red Sea,
          that made you hurry out of their way?
      What happened, Jordan River, that you turned away?
      Why, mountains, did you skip like rams?
      Why, hills, like lambs?"

At Your presence, Lord, the earth trembled,
    at Your presence, O God of Jacob.
You turned the rock into a pool of water;
    Yes, a spring of water flowed from solid rock.

Your presence causes the whole earth to tremble.

115

Not to me, O LORD, not to me,
    but to Your name I give glory,
    because of Your lovingkindness, because of Your truth.
Why should the nations say,
    "Where, now, is their God?"

But You, my God, are in the heavens;
    You do whatever You please.
Their idols are silver and gold,
    the work of man's hands.

They have mouths, but they cannot speak.
They have eyes, but they cannot see.
They have ears, but they cannot hear.
They have noses, but they cannot smell.
They have hands, but they cannot feel.
They have feet, but they cannot walk.
They cannot make a sound with their throat.
Those who make them will become like them,
    everyone who trusts in them.

As the psalmist pleaded with Israel to trust in You,
    for You were their help and their shield,
    give me the courage to trust in You.
As he pleaded with the house of Aaron to trust in You,
    for You were their help and their shield,
    give me the courage to trust in You.

You are worthy of all glory.

Give me the courage to fear You, O Lord,
and to trust in You.
You are my help and my shield.
You have been mindful of me; You will bless me.
You will bless the house of Israel.
You will bless the house of Aaron.
You will bless those who fear You,
the small together with the great.

Lord, give me increase, me and my children.
Bless me, O Lord, maker of heaven and earth.

The heavens are Your heavens,
but the earth You have given to the sons of men.
The dead do not praise You,
nor do any who go down into silence.
But as for me, I will bless You, Lord,
from this time forth and forever.

I praise You, Lord!

You are my help and my shield.
You will bless me.

116

I love You, LORD, because You hear my voice
   and my prayer for mercy.
Because You bend down to listen,
   I will call upon You as long as I live.
Even if death wraps its ropes around me
   or the terrors of the grave overtake me.
Even when I see only trouble and sorrow,
   I will call on Your name: "Please, LORD, save me!"

How kind You are! How good You are!
   So merciful are You, my God!
You protect those of childlike faith;
   I was facing death, and You saved me.
Let my soul be at rest again, for You have been good to me.

You have saved me from death,
   my eyes from tears, my feet from stumbling.
And so I walk in Your presence as I live here on earth!
I believed in You, so I said,
   "I am deeply troubled, LORD."
In my anxiety, I cried out to You,
   "These people are all liars!"

You hear me.
You are kind.
You are good.
You are merciful.
You protect those of childlike faith.
You have been good to me.
You have saved me from death.

What can I offer You, Lord
    for all You have done for me?
I will lift up the cup of salvation
    and praise Your name for saving me.
I will keep my promises to You, O Lord,
    in the presence of all Your people.
You care deeply when Your loved ones die.

O Lord, I am Your servant;
    Yes, I am Your servant, born into Your household;
    You have freed me from my chains.
I will offer You a sacrifice of thanksgiving
    and call on Your name.
I will fulfill my vows to You, O Lord,
    in the presence of all Your people—
    in Your house, O Lord.

I praise You Lord!

You have freed me from my chains.

117

May all the nations praise You, LORD.

May all the people of the earth praise You.

For Your unfailing love for me is powerful;
    Your faithfulness endures forever.

I praise You, LORD!

Your unfailing love for me is powerful.
Your faithfulness endures forever.

118

I give thanks to You, LORD, for You are good!
Your faithful love endures forever.
Let all Israel repeat: "His faithful love endures forever."
Let Aaron's descendants, the priests, repeat:
    "His faithful love endures forever."
Let all who fear You repeat:
    "His faithful love endures forever."

In my distress, I pray to You, LORD,
    and You answer me and set me free.
You are for me, so I will have no fear.
What can man do to me?
Yes, You are for me; You will help me.
I will look in triumph at those who hate me.
It is better to take refuge in You than to trust in people.
It is better to take refuge in You than to trust in princes.
Though hostile forces surrounded me,
    in Your name, I overcame them.
Yes, they surrounded and attacked me,
    but, in Your name, I overcame them.
They swarmed around me like bees;
    They blazed against me like a crackling fire,
    but, in Your name, I overcame them.
I was pushed hard, so that I was falling, but You rescued me.
You are my strength and my song;
    You have given me victory.

You are good.
Your love endures forever.
You answer me and set me free.
You are for me, and You will help me.
You are my strength and my song.
You give me victory.

Songs of joy and victory are sung in the camp of the godly.
Your strong right arm has done glorious things!
Your strong right arm is raised in triumph.
Your strong right arm has done glorious things!
I will not die; Instead, I will live to tell what You have done.
You have punished me severely, but You did not let me die.
Open for me the gates where the righteous enter,
  and I will go in and thank You.
These gates lead to Your presence, LORD,
  and the godly enter there.
I thank You for answering my prayer and giving me victory!

The stone that the builders rejected
  has now become the cornerstone.
This is Your doing, and it is wonderful to see.
This is the day You have made.
I will rejoice and be glad in it.
Please, LORD, save me.
Please, LORD, give me success.

Bless those who come in Your name.
Bless those from Your house.
You are God, and You have given me light.
Please, LORD, receive with joy my sacrifices to You.

You are my God, and I will praise You!
You are my God, and I will exalt You!
I give thanks to You, for You are good!
Your faithful love endures forever.

You are the creator of each day.
You are my God.
You are good.
Your love endures forever.

119

You tell me I will be blessed, if my way is blameless
    and if I follow Your instructions, LORD.
You tell me I will be blessed, if I obey Your laws,
    if I search for You with all my heart,
    if I do not compromise with evil,
    and if I walk only in Your paths.
You have charged me to keep Your commandments carefully.
Oh, that my actions would consistently reflect Your decrees!
Then I will not be ashamed
    when I compare my life with Your commands.
As I learn Your righteous regulations,
    I will thank You by living as I should!
I will obey Your decrees. Please don't give up on me!

How can I keep my way pure? By obeying Your word.
I have tried hard to find You—
    don't let me wander from Your commands.
I have hidden Your word in my heart,
    that I might not sin against You.
I praise You, O LORD; Teach me Your decrees.
I have recited aloud all the regulations You have given me.
I have rejoiced in Your laws as much as in riches.
I will study Your commandments and reflect on Your ways.
I will delight in Your decrees and not forget Your word.

Your Word is good.

Be good to Your servant, that I may live and obey Your word.
Open my eyes to see
the wonderful truths in Your instructions.
I am only a foreigner in the land.
Don't hide Your commands from me!
I am always overwhelmed with a desire for Your regulations.
You rebuke the arrogant;
Those who wander from Your commands are cursed.
Don't let them scorn and insult me,
for I have obeyed Your laws.
Even princes sit and speak against me,
but I will meditate on Your decrees.
Your laws please me; They give me wise advice.

I lie in the dust; Revive me by Your word.
I told You my plans, and You answered.
Now teach me Your decrees.
Help me understand the meaning of Your precepts,
and I will meditate on Your wonderful deeds.
I weep with sorrow; Encourage me by Your word.
Keep me from lying to myself;
Give me the privilege of knowing Your instructions.
I have chosen to be faithful;
I have determined to live by Your regulations.
I cling to Your laws. LORD, don't let me be put to shame!
I will pursue Your commands,
for You expand my understanding.

Your Word is good.

Teach me Your decrees, O Lord; I will keep them to the end.
Give me understanding, that I may obey Your law
	and keep it with all my heart.
Make me walk in the path of Your commands,
	for that is where my happiness is found.
Give me an eagerness for Your laws
	rather than a love for money!
Turn my eyes from worthless things,
	and give me life through Your word.
Reassure me of Your promise, made to those who fear You.
Help me abandon my shameful ways;
	For Your regulations are good.

I long to obey Your commandments!
Renew my life with Your goodness.
Lord, give me Your unfailing love,
	the salvation that You promised me.
Then I can answer those who taunt me,
	for I trust in Your word.
Do not snatch Your word of truth from me,
	for Your regulations are my only hope.
I will keep on obeying Your instructions forever and ever.
I will walk in freedom,
	for I have devoted myself to Your commandments.
I will speak to kings about Your laws,
	and I will not be ashamed.
How I delight in Your commands! How I love them!
I honor and love Your commands.
I meditate on Your decrees.

Your Word is good.

Remember Your promise to me; It is my only hope.
Your promise revives me; It comforts me in all my troubles.
The proud hold me in utter contempt,
    but I do not turn away from Your instructions.
I meditate on Your age-old regulations;
    O LORD, they comfort me.
I become furious with the wicked,
    because they reject Your instructions.
Your decrees have been the theme of my songs
    wherever I have lived.
I reflect at night on who You are, O LORD;
    Therefore, I obey Your instructions.
This is how I spend my life: obeying Your commandments.

LORD, You are mine! I promise to obey Your words!
With all my heart I want Your blessings.
Be merciful as You promised.
I pondered the direction of my life,
    and I turned to follow Your laws.
I will hurry, without delay, to obey Your commands.
Evil people try to drag me into sin,
    but I am firmly anchored to Your instructions.
I rise at midnight to thank You for Your just regulations.
I am a friend to anyone who fears You—
    anyone who obeys Your commandments.
O LORD, Your unfailing love fills the earth;
    Teach me Your decrees.

Your Word is good.

You have done many good things for me, LORD,
    just as You promised.
I believe in Your commands;
    Now teach me good judgment and knowledge.
I used to wander off until You disciplined me;
    But now I closely follow Your word.
You are good and do only good; Teach me Your decrees.
Arrogant people smear me with lies,
    but in truth I obey Your commandments with all my heart.
Their hearts are dull and stupid,
    but I delight in Your instructions.
My suffering was good for me,
    for it taught me to pay attention to Your decrees.
Your instructions are more valuable to me
    than millions in gold and silver.

You made me; You created me.
Now give me the sense to follow Your commands
May all who fear You find in me a cause for joy,
    for I have put my hope in Your word.
I know, O LORD, that Your regulations are fair;
    You disciplined me because I needed it.
Now let Your unfailing love comfort me,
    just as You promised me, Your servant.
Surround me with Your tender mercies so I may live,
    for Your instructions are my delight.
May the arrogant, who lied about me, be ashamed;
    Meanwhile, I will meditate on Your precepts.
Let me be united with all who fear You,
    with those who know Your laws.
May I be blameless in keeping Your decrees;
    Then I will never be ashamed.

Your Word is good.

I am worn out waiting for Your rescue,
>but I have put my hope in Your word.

My eyes are straining to see Your promises come true.
When will You comfort me?

I am shriveled like a wineskin in the smoke,
>but I have not forgotten to obey Your decrees.

How long must I wait?
When will You punish those who persecute me?

These arrogant people who hate Your instructions
>have dug deep pits to trap me.

All Your commands are trustworthy.
Protect me from those who hunt me down without cause.

They almost finished me off,
>but I refused to abandon Your commandments.

In Your unfailing love, spare my life;
>Then I can continue to obey Your laws.

Your eternal word, O LORD, stands firm in heaven.
Your faithfulness extends to every generation,
>as enduring as the earth You created.

Your regulations remain true to this day,
>for everything serves Your plans.

If Your instructions hadn't sustained me with joy,
>I would have died in my misery.

I will never forget Your commandments,
>for by them You give me life.

I am Yours; Rescue me!
For I have worked hard at obeying Your commandments.
Though the wicked hide along the way to kill me,
>I will quietly keep my mind on Your laws.

Even perfection has its limits,
>but Your commands have no limit.

Your Word is good.

Oh, how I love Your instructions!
I think about them all day long.
Your commands make me wiser than my enemies,
  for they are my constant guide.
Yes, I have more insight than my teachers,
  for I am always thinking of Your laws.
I am even wiser than my elders,
  for I have kept Your commandments.
I have refused to walk on any evil path,
  so that I may remain obedient to Your word.
I haven't turned away from Your regulations,
  for You have taught me well.
How sweet Your words taste to me;
  They are sweeter than honey.
Your commandments give me understanding;
  No wonder I hate every false way of life.

Your word is a lamp to guide my feet and a light for my path.
I've promised it once, and I'll promise it again:
  I will obey Your righteous regulations.
I have suffered much, O Lord;
  Restore my life again as You promised.
Lord, accept my offering of praise,
  and teach me Your regulations.
My life constantly hangs in the balance,
  but I will not stop obeying Your instructions.
The wicked have set their traps for me,
  but I will not turn from Your commandments.
Your laws are my treasure; They are my heart's delight.
I am determined to keep Your decrees to the very end.

Your Word is good.

I hate those with divided loyalties,
  but I love Your instructions.
You are my refuge and my shield;
  Your word is my source of hope.
I will say, "Get out of my life, you evil-minded people,
  for I intend to obey the commands of my God."
LORD, sustain me as You promised, that I may live!
Do not let my hope be crushed.
Sustain me, and I will be rescued;
  Then I will meditate continually on Your decrees.
But You have rejected all who stray from Your decrees.
They are only fooling themselves.
You skim off the wicked of the earth like scum;
  No wonder I love to obey Your laws!
I tremble in fear of You; I stand in awe of Your regulations.

Don't leave me to the mercy of my enemies,
  for I have done what is just and right.
Please guarantee a blessing for me.
Don't let the arrogant oppress me!
My eyes strain to see Your rescue,
  to see the truth of Your promise fulfilled.
I am Your servant; Deal with me in unfailing love,
  and teach me Your decrees.
Give discernment to me, Your servant;
  Then I will understand Your laws.
LORD, it is time for You to act,
  for these evil people have violated Your instructions.
Truly, I love Your commands more than gold,
  even the finest gold.
Each of Your commandments is right.
That is why I hate every false way.

Your Word is good.

Your laws are wonderful. No wonder I obey them!
The teaching of Your word gives light,
    so even the simple can understand.
I pant with expectation, longing for Your commands.
Come and show me Your mercy,
    as You do for all who love Your name.
Guide my steps by Your word,
    so I will not be overcome by evil.
Ransom me from the oppression of evil people;
    Then I can obey Your commandments.
Look upon me with love; Teach me Your decrees.
Rivers of tears gush from my eyes
    because people disobey Your instructions.

O Lord, You are righteous, and Your regulations are fair.
Your laws are perfect and completely trustworthy.
I am overwhelmed with indignation,
    for my enemies have disregarded Your words.
Your promises have been thoroughly tested;
    That is why I love them so much.
I am insignificant and despised,
    but I don't forget Your commandments.
Your justice is eternal,
    and Your instructions are perfectly true.
As pressure and stress bear down on me,
    I find joy in Your commands.
Your laws are always right;
    Help me to understand them so I may live.

Your Word is good.

I pray with all my heart; Answer me, Lord!
I will obey Your decrees.
I cry out to You; Rescue me, that I may obey Your laws.
I rise early, before the sun is up;
    I cry out for help and put my hope in Your words.
I stay awake through the night, thinking about Your promise.
In Your faithful love, O Lord, hear my cry;
    Let me be revived by following Your regulations.
Lawless people are coming to attack me;
    They live far from Your instructions.
But You are near, O Lord, and all Your commands are true.
I have known from my earliest days
    that Your laws will last forever.

Look upon my suffering and rescue me,
    for I have not forgotten Your instructions.
Argue my case; Take my side!
Protect my life as You promised.
The wicked are far from rescue,
    for they do not bother with Your decrees.
Lord, how great is Your mercy;
    Let me be revived by following Your regulations.
Many persecute and trouble me,
    yet I have not swerved from Your laws.
Seeing these traitors makes me sick at heart,
    because they care nothing for Your word.
See how I love Your commandments, Lord.
Give back my life because of Your unfailing love.
The very essence of Your words is truth;
    All Your just regulations will stand forever.

Your Word is good.

Powerful people harass me without cause,
    but my heart trembles only at Your word.
I rejoice in Your word
    like one who discovers a great treasure.
I hate and abhor all falsehood, but I love Your instructions.
I will praise You seven times a day
    because all Your regulations are just.
Those who love Your instructions have great peace
    and do not stumble.
I long for Your rescue, LORD,
    so I have obeyed Your commands.
I have obeyed Your laws, for I love them very much.
Yes, I obey Your commandments and laws
    because You know everything I do.

O LORD, listen to my cry;
    Give me the discerning mind You promised.
Listen to my prayer; Rescue me as You promised.
Let praise flow from my lips,
    for You have taught me Your decrees.
Let my tongue sing about Your word,
    for all Your commands are right.
Give me a helping hand,
    for I have chosen to follow Your commandments.
O LORD, I have longed for Your rescue,
    and Your instructions are my delight.
Let me live so I can praise You,
    and may Your regulations help me.
I have wandered away like a lost sheep;
    Come and find me,
    for I have not forgotten Your commands.

Your Word is good.

120

I bring my troubles to You, LORD.
I cry out to You, and You answer my prayer.
Rescue me, O LORD, from liars and from all deceitful people.
What will You do to those who deceive with their tongues?
Will You severely punish them?
You have told me that You will pierce them
    with sharp arrows and burn them with glowing coals.

How I suffer, living in this broken world.
I am tired of living among people who hate peace.
I search for peace; But when I speak of peace, they want war!

You answer my prayer.
You will punish the wicked.

121

I look up to the mountains;
    From where does my help come?
My help comes from You, LORD,
    who made heaven and earth!

You will not let me stumble;
    You, who watches over me, will not slumber.
Indeed, You, who watches over Israel,
    never slumbers or sleeps.

You watch over me!
You stand beside me as my protective shade.
The sun will not harm me by day, nor the moon at night.

You keep me from all harm and watch over my life.
You keep watch over me as I come and go,
    both now and forever.

You made heaven and earth.
You will not let me stumble.
You watch over me.
You never sleep.
You stand beside me.
You keep me from all harm.
You keep watch over me.

122

The psalmist was glad when those around him said,
    "Let me go to the house of the LORD."

While he was there, standing inside Jerusalem's gates,
    he noted:

-   that it was a well-built city,
      with seamless walls that could not be breached;
-   that all the tribes of Israel—Your people—
      made their pilgrimage there,
      to give thanks to Your name,
      as the law required of them; and
-   that in Jerusalem stood the thrones
      where judgment was given,
      the thrones of the dynasty of David.

I pray for peace in Jerusalem.
May all who love it prosper.

May there be peace within its walls
    and prosperity in its palaces.

For the sake of my family and friends,
    I will say, "May Jerusalem have peace."

For the sake of Your house, O LORD, my God,
    I will seek what is best for Jerusalem.

You love Jerusalem.

123

I lift my eyes to You, O God, the One enthroned in heaven.
I keep looking to You, my God, for Your mercy,
    just as servants keep their eyes on their master,
    as a slave girl watches her mistress for the slightest signal.

Have mercy on me, LORD, have mercy,
    for I have had my fill of contempt.
I have had more than my fill of the scoffing of the proud
    and the contempt of the arrogant.

You are enthroned in heaven.
You give mercy.

124

What if You were not on my side?
What if You were not on my side when people attacked me?
They would have swallowed me alive in their burning anger.
The waters would have engulfed me;
    The current would have overwhelmed me.
Yes, the raging waters of their fury
    would have overwhelmed my very life.

I praise You, LORD,
    who did not let their teeth tear me apart!
I escaped like a bird from a hunter's trap.
The trap is broken, and I am free!
My help is from You, LORD, who made heaven and earth.

You are on my side.
You made heaven and earth.

125

Those who trust in You, Lord, are as secure as Mount Zion;
    They will not be defeated but will endure forever.
Just as the mountains surround Jerusalem,
    so You surround Your people, both now and forever.
The wicked will not rule the land of the godly,
    for then the godly might be tempted to do wrong.

O Lord, do good to those who are good,
    whose hearts are in tune with You.
But banish those who turn to crooked ways, O Lord.
Take them away with those who do evil.
May Israel have peace!

You surround me.

126

When the LORD brought back his exiles to Jerusalem,
    it was like a dream.
They were filled with laughter, and they sang for joy.
And the other nations said,
    "What amazing things the LORD has done for them."
And You had done amazing things for them,
    and they were glad.
You have done amazing things for me, LORD, and I am glad!

Restore my well-being, LORD,
    as streams renew the desert.
You tell me that those who plant in tears
    will harvest with shouts of joy
      and that they who weep as they go to plant their seed
      will sing as they return with the harvest.

Restore my well-being, LORD.

You do amazing things for me.

127

Unless You build the house,
    they work in vain who build it.
Unless You guard the city,
    the watchman keeps awake in vain.
It is useless for me to work so hard,
    from early morning until late at night,
    anxiously working for food to eat;
    For You give to me, Your beloved, even in my sleep.

My children are a gift from You;
    They are a reward from You.
My children are like arrows in a warrior's hands.
I am so blessed to have a quiver full of them!
I will not be put to shame
    when I confront my accusers at the city gates.

You are my provider.

128

How joyful are those who fear You, Lord—
    all who follow Your ways!

You tell me that I will enjoy the fruit of my labor;
    that I will be joyful and prosperous;
    that I will be like a fruitful grapevine,
    flourishing within my home;
    that my children will be like vigorous young olive trees,
    as they sit around my table;
    that this is Your blessing for those who fear You.

Lord, please continue to bless me.
May I see Jerusalem prosper as long as I live.
May I live to enjoy my grandchildren.
May Israel have peace!

You bless those who fear You.

129

From my earliest youth my enemies have persecuted me,
    but they have never defeated me.
My back is covered with cuts,
    as if a farmer had plowed upon my back.
But You are good, Lord;
    You have cut me free from the ropes of the ungodly.

May all who hate Jerusalem
    be turned back in shameful defeat.
May they be as useless as grass on a rooftop,
    which withers before it grows up,
    ignored by the harvester,
    despised by the binder.

Though those who pass by
    may refuse to give them this blessing:
    "The Lord bless you; I bless you in the Lord's name."

LORD, give me the courage and compassion
    to ask You to bless my enemies with salvation.

You are good.

130

From the depths of despair, O LORD, I call for Your help.
Hear my cry, O Lord.
Pay attention to my prayer.
LORD, if You kept a record of my sins,
    who, O Lord, could ever survive?
But You offer forgiveness, that I might learn to fear You.

I am counting on You, LORD; Yes, I am counting on You.
I have put my hope in Your word.
I long for You more than sentries long for the dawn,
    yes, more than sentries long for the dawn.

I hope in You, LORD; For with You there is unfailing love.
Your redemption overflows.
You will redeem Israel from every kind of sin.

You keep no record of my sins.
You offer forgiveness.
You love me with unfailing love.
Your redemption overflows.

131

LORD, my heart is not proud; My eyes are not haughty.
I don't concern myself with matters too great
    or too awesome for me to grasp.
Instead, I have calmed and quieted myself,
    like a weaned child
    who no longer cries for its mother's milk.

Yes, like a weaned child is my soul within me.
I put my hope in You, LORD—now and always.

You are my hope.

132

LORD, remember David and all that he suffered.
He made a solemn promise to You.
He vowed to You, the Mighty One of Israel:

> "I will not go home; I will not let myself rest.
> I will not let my eyes sleep nor close my eyelids in slumber
>   until I find a place to build a house for the LORD,
>   a sanctuary for the Mighty One of Israel."

Israel heard that the Ark was in Ephrathah;
    Then they found it in the distant countryside of Jaar.

As they went to Your dwelling place, LORD,
    let me come before You;
    Let me worship at the footstool of Your throne.

As they asked You to arise and enter Your resting place,
    along with the Ark, the symbol of Your power,
    and that Your priests would be clothed in godliness
    and that Your loyal servants would sing for joy,
    let me, likewise, be clothed in godliness and sing for joy.

For the sake of Your servant David,
    do not reject Your chosen king.
You swore an oath to David
    with a promise You will never take back:

> "I will place one of your descendants on your throne.
> If your descendants obey the terms of My covenant
>   and the laws that I teach them,
>   then your royal line will continue forever and ever."

You make eternal promises.

For You chose Jerusalem; You desired it for Your home.
You said:

"This is My resting place forever.
I will live here, for this is the home I desired.
I will bless this city and make it prosperous;
    I will satisfy its poor with food.
I will clothe its priests with godliness;
    Its faithful servants will sing for joy.
Here I will increase the power of David;
    My anointed one will be a light for My people.
I will clothe his enemies with shame,
    but he will be a glorious king."

You make eternal promises.

133

How wonderful and pleasant it is
for brothers live together in harmony!

For harmony is as precious as the anointing oil
that was poured over Aaron's head,
that ran down his beard and onto the border of his robe.

Harmony is as refreshing as the dew from Mount Hermon
that falls on the mountains of Zion.

And there You pronounced Your blessing, eternal life.

You give eternal life.

134

I praise You, LORD, as one of Your servants.

I lift up my hands to You and praise You.

Bless me, LORD, You who made heaven and earth.

> *You are praiseworthy.*
> *You made heaven and earth.*

135

I praise You, LORD!
I praise Your name!

I praise You, as one of Your servants,
    like those who served in Your house,
    in the courts of the Your house.

I praise You, LORD, for You are good;
    I will celebrate Your lovely name with music.

You chose Jacob for Yourself,
    Israel for Your own special treasure.
I know Your greatness, LORD—
    that You are greater than any other god.
You do whatever You please,
    throughout all heaven and earth,
    and on the seas and in their depths.
You cause the clouds to rise over the whole earth.
You send the lightning with the rain
    and release the wind from Your storehouses.
You destroyed the firstborn in each Egyptian home,
    both people and animals.
You performed miraculous signs and wonders in Egypt
    against Pharaoh and all his people.
You struck down great nations
    and slaughtered mighty kings—
    Sihon king of the Amorites,
    Og king of Bashan, and all the kings of Canaan.

> *You are praiseworthy.*
> *You are good.*
> *You are greater than any other god.*
> *You do whatever You please.*

You gave their land as an inheritance,
a special possession to Your people Israel.
Your name, O Lord, endures forever;
Your fame, O Lord, is known to every generation.
For You will give justice to Your people
and have compassion on Your servants.

The idols of the nations are merely things of silver and gold,
shaped by human hands.
They have mouths but cannot speak, and eyes but cannot see.
They have ears but cannot hear,
and mouths but cannot breathe.
And those who make idols are just like them,
as are all who trust in them.

May Israel praise You, Lord!
May the priests—descendants of Aaron—praise You, Lord!
May the Levites, praise You, Lord!
May all who fear You, praise You, Lord!
May You, who lives in Jerusalem, be praised from Zion.

I praise You, Lord!

> *Your name endures forever.*
> *You will give justice to Your people.*
> *You will have compassion on Your servants.*

136

I give thanks to You, LORD, for You are good!
Your faithful love endures forever.

I give thanks to You, the God of gods.
Your faithful love endures forever.

I give thanks to You, the Lord of lords.
Your faithful love endures forever.

I give thanks to You, who alone does mighty miracles.
Your faithful love endures forever.

I give thanks to You, who made the heavens so skillfully.
Your faithful love endures forever.

I give thanks to You, who placed the earth among the waters.
Your faithful love endures forever.

I give thanks to You, who made the heavenly lights—
Your faithful love endures forever.

the sun to rule the day,
Your faithful love endures forever.

and the moon and stars to rule the night.
Your faithful love endures forever.

I give thanks to You, who killed the firstborn of Egypt.
Your faithful love endures forever.

> *You are good.*
> *You alone do mighty miracles.*
> *You made the heavens.*
> *Your faithful love endures forever.*

You brought Israel out of Egypt.
Your faithful love endures forever.

You acted with a strong hand and powerful arm.
Your faithful love endures forever.

I give thanks to You, who parted the Red Sea.
Your faithful love endures forever.

You led Israel safely through,
Your faithful love endures forever.

but You hurled Pharaoh and his army into the Red Sea.
Your faithful love endures forever.

I give thanks to You,
who led Your people through the wilderness.
Your faithful love endures forever.

I give thanks to You, who struck down mighty kings.
Your faithful love endures forever.

You killed powerful kings—
Your faithful love endures forever.

Sihon, king of the Amorites,
Your faithful love endures forever.

and Og, king of Bashan.
Your faithful love endures forever.

You brought Israel out of Egypt.
Your faithful love endures forever.

You gave the land of these kings as an inheritance—
Your faithful love endures forever.

a special possession to Your servant Israel.
Your faithful love endures forever.

You remembered me in my weakness.
Your faithful love endures forever.

You saved me from my enemies.
Your faithful love endures forever.

You give food to every living thing.
Your faithful love endures forever.

I give thanks to You, the God of heaven.
Your faithful love endures forever.

You remembered me in my weakness.
You saved me from my enemies.
You give food to every living thing.
Your faithful love endures forever.

137

Your people sat and wept by the rivers of Babylon,
    as they thought of Jerusalem.
They put away their harps,
    hanging them on the branches of poplar trees.
For their captors demanded a song from them.
Their tormentors insisted on a joyful hymn, saying:
    "Sing me one of those songs of Jerusalem!"

Your people said:

    "How can we sing the songs of the LORD
        while in a pagan land?
    If I forget you, O Jerusalem,
        let my right hand forget how to play the harp.
    May my tongue stick to the roof of my mouth
        if I fail to remember you,
        if I don't make Jerusalem my greatest joy.

    O LORD, remember what the Edomites did
        on the day the armies of Babylon captured Jerusalem.
    'Destroy it!' they yelled. 'Level it to the ground!'

    O Babylon, you will be destroyed.
    Happy is the one who pays you back
        for what you have done to me.
    Happy is the one who takes your babies
        and smashes them against the rocks!"

O LORD, may I not fail to remember You;
    May You always be my greatest joy.

You will execute justice.

138

I give You thanks, O LORD, with all my heart;
    I will sing Your praises before the gods.
I bow before Your holy temple as I worship.
I praise Your name, for Your unfailing love and faithfulness;
    For Your promises are backed
    by all the honor of Your name.
As soon as I pray, You answer me;
    You encourage me by giving me strength.

Every king in all the earth will thank You, LORD,
    for all of them will hear Your words.
Yes, they will sing about Your ways,
    for Your glory is very great.
Though You are great, You care for the humble,
    but You keep Your distance from the proud.

Your love is unfailing.
Your promises are backed by Your name.
You answer me.
You encourage me.
You give me strength.
Your glory is very great.
You are great.
You care for the humble.
You keep Your distance from the proud.

Though I am surrounded by troubles,
    You will protect me from the anger of my enemies.
You reach out Your hand,
    and the power of Your right hand saves me.
You will work out Your plans for my life—
    for Your faithful love, O Lord, endures forever.
Don't abandon me, for You made me.

You will protect me.
You will work out Your plans for my life.
Your love endures forever.
You made me.

139

O Lord, You have searched me and known me.
You know when I sit down and when I rise up;
    You understand my thought from afar.
You scrutinize my path and my lying down,
    and are intimately acquainted with all my ways.

Even before there is a word on my tongue,
    behold, O Lord, You know it all.
You have enclosed me behind and before,
    and laid Your hand upon me.
Such knowledge is too wonderful for me;
    It is too high, I cannot attain to it.

Where can I go from Your Spirit?
Or where can I flee from Your presence?
If I ascend to heaven, You are there;
    If I make my bed in Sheol, behold, You are there.
If I take the wings of the dawn,
    if I dwell in the remotest part of the sea,
    even there Your hand will lead me,
    and Your right hand will lay hold of me.

If I say, "Surely the darkness will overwhelm me,
    and the light around me will be night,"
Even the darkness is not dark to You,
    and the night is as bright as the day.
Darkness and light are alike to You.

You know me.
You understand my thoughts.
You are intimately acquainted with all my ways.
You know everything.
You are everywhere.

For You formed my inward parts;
　　You wove me in my mother's womb.
I will give thanks to You,
　　for I am fearfully and wonderfully made.
Wonderful are Your works, and my soul knows it very well.

My frame was not hidden from You
　　when I was made in secret
　　and skillfully wrought in the depths of the earth.
Your eyes have seen my unformed substance;
　　And in Your book were all written
　　the days that were ordained for me,
　　when as yet there was not one of them.

How precious also are Your thoughts to me, O God!
How vast is the sum of them!
If I should count them, they would outnumber the sand.

When I awake, I am still with You.
At times I want You to slay the wicked, O God,
　　and to make the men of bloodshed depart from me;
　　For they speak against You wickedly,
　　and Your enemies take Your name in vain.

Should I not hate those who hate You, O Lord?
And should I not loathe those who rise up against You?
At times, I hate them with the utmost hatred;
　　They have become my enemies.
But You tell me to love them and pray for them.
Search me, O God, and know my heart;
　　Try me and know my anxious thoughts;
　　And see if there be any hurtful way in me,
　　and lead me in the everlasting way.

You created me with great care.
You control everything.

140

O Lord, rescue me from evil people.
Protect me from those who are violent,
    those who plot evil in their hearts
    and stir up trouble all day long.
Their tongues sting like a snake;
    the venom of a viper drips from their lips.

O Lord, keep me out of the hands of the wicked.
Protect me from those who are violent,
    for they are plotting against me.
The proud have set a trap to catch me;
    They have stretched out a net;
    They have placed traps all along the way.

You are my God!
Listen, O Lord, to my cries for mercy!
O Sovereign Lord, the strong one who rescues me,
    You protect me in the day of battle.
Lord, do not let evil people have their way.
Do not let their evil schemes succeed,
    or they will become proud.

Lord, I want to say:

    "Let my enemies be destroyed
        by the very evil they have planned for me.
    Let burning coals fall down on their heads.
    Let them be thrown into the fire
        or into watery pits from which they can't escape.
    Don't let liars prosper here in my land.
    Cause great disasters to fall on the violent."

You are my God.

But You tell me to love my enemies
 and to pray for those who persecute me;
 And I trust You.
For I know You will help those they persecute;
 You will give justice to the poor.
Surely righteous people are praising Your name;
 And the godly will live in Your presence.

You protect me.
You give justice to the poor.

141

O Lord, I am calling to You. Please hurry!
  Listen when I cry to You for help!
Accept my prayer as incense offered to You,
  and my upraised hands as an evening offering.

Take control of what I say, O Lord,
  and guard my lips.
Don't let me drift toward evil
  or take part in acts of wickedness.
Don't let me share in the delicacies
  of those who do wrong.

Let the godly strike me;
  It will be a kindness.
If they correct me, it is soothing medicine;
  Don't let me refuse it.

But I pray constantly
  against the wicked and their deeds.
When their leaders are thrown down from a cliff,
  the wicked will listen to my words and find them true.
Like rocks brought up by a plow,
  the bones of the wicked will lie scattered without burial.

I look to You for help, O Sovereign Lord.
You are my refuge; Don't let them kill me.
Keep me from the traps they have set for me,
  from the snares of those who do wrong.
Let the wicked fall into their own nets,
  but let me escape.

You are my refuge.

142

I cry out to You, LORD;
    I plead for Your mercy.
I pour out my complaints before You
    and tell You all my troubles.
When I am overwhelmed,
    You alone know the way I should turn.
Wherever I go,
    my enemies have set traps for me.

I look for someone to come and help me,
    but it seems like no one gives me a passing thought,
    like no one will help me,
    like no one cares a bit what happens to me.

So I cry out to You, O LORD.
I say:

    "You are my place of refuge.
    You are all I really want in life.
    Hear my cry, for I am very low.
    Rescue me from my persecutors,
        for they are too strong for me.
    Bring my soul out of prison so I can thank You.
    The godly will surround me, for You are good to me."

You alone know my path.
You are my place of refuge.
You are good to me.

143

Hear my prayer, O LORD; Listen to my plea!
Answer me because You are faithful and righteous.
Don't put Your servant on trial,
    for no one is innocent before You.
My enemy has chased me.
He has knocked me to the ground
    and forces me to live in darkness like those in the grave.
I am losing all hope; I am paralyzed with fear.
I remember the days of old.
I ponder all Your great works
    and think about what You have done.
I lift my hands to You in prayer.
I thirst for You as parched land thirsts for rain.

Come quickly, LORD, and answer me,
    for my depression deepens.
Don't turn away from me, or I will die.
Let me hear of Your unfailing love each morning,
    for I am trusting You.
Show me where to walk, for I give myself to You.
Rescue me from my enemies, LORD;
    I run to You to hide me.
Teach me to do Your will, for You are my God.
May Your gracious Spirit lead me forward
    on a firm footing.
For the glory of Your name, O LORD, preserve my life.
Because of Your faithfulness, bring me out of this distress.
In Your unfailing love, silence all my enemies
    and subdue all my foes, for I am Your servant.

> *You are faithful and righteous.*
> *Your love is unfailing.*
> *You are my God.*
> *Your Spirit leads me.*

144

I praise You, LORD, my rock.
You train my hands for war
    and give my fingers skill for battle.
You are my loving ally and my fortress,
    my tower of safety, my rescuer.
You are my shield, and I take refuge in You.
You subdue people under me.

O LORD, what are human beings that You should notice them,
    mere mortals that You should think about them?
For they are like a breath of air;
    Their days are like a passing shadow.
Open the heavens, LORD, and come down.
Touch the mountains so they billow smoke.
Hurl Your lightning bolts and scatter Your enemies!
Shoot Your arrows and confuse them!
Reach down from heaven and rescue me;
    Rescue me from deep waters,
    from the power of my enemies.

Their mouths are full of lies;
    They swear to tell the truth, but they lie instead.
I will sing a new song to You, O God!
I will sing Your praises.
For You grant victory to kings!
You rescued Your servant David from the fatal sword.
Save me and rescue me from the power of my enemies.
Their mouths are full of lies;
    They swear to tell the truth, but they lie instead.

You are my ally, my fortress, and my tower of safety.
You are my rescuer, my shield, and my refuge.

As David asked that Israel's sons
    would flourish in their youth,
    like well-nurtured plants;
    that their daughters would be like graceful pillars,
    carved to beautify a palace;
    that their barns would be filled with crops of every kind;
    that the flocks in their fields
    would multiply by the thousands,
    even tens of thousands;
    that their oxen would be loaded down with produce; and
    that there would be no enemy breaking through their walls,
    no going into captivity, and
    no cries of alarm in their town squares,
    LORD, please provide for me in such ways.

Yes, joyful are those who live like this!
Joyful indeed are those who make You their God.

You give joy.

145

I will exalt You, my God and King,
    and praise Your name forever and ever.
I will praise You every day; Yes, I will praise You forever.
Great are You, LORD! You are most worthy of praise!
No one can measure Your greatness.

Let each generation tell its children of Your mighty acts;
    Let them proclaim Your power.
I will meditate on Your majestic, glorious splendor
    and Your wonderful miracles.
Your awe-inspiring deeds will be on every tongue;
    I will proclaim Your greatness.
Everyone will share the story of Your wonderful goodness;
    They will sing with joy about Your righteousness.

You are merciful and compassionate,
    slow to get angry and filled with unfailing love.
You are good to everyone.
You shower compassion on all Your creation.
All of Your works will thank You, LORD,
    and Your faithful followers will praise You.
They will speak of the glory of Your kingdom;
    They will give examples of Your power.
They will tell about Your mighty deeds
    and about the majesty and glory of Your reign.

You are great.
You are most worthy of praise.
You are merciful and compassionate.
You are slow to get angry.
You are filled with unfailing love.
You are good to everyone.
You shower compassion on all Your creation.

For Your kingdom is an everlasting kingdom.
You rule throughout all generations.
You always keep Your promises;
    You are gracious in all You do.
You help the fallen and lift those bent beneath their loads.

The eyes of all look to You in hope;
    You give them their food as they need it.
When You open Your hand,
    You satisfy the hunger and thirst of every living thing.
You are righteous in everything You do;
    You are filled with kindness.
You are close to all who call on You,
    yes, to all who call on You in truth.
You grant the desires of those who fear You;
    You hear their cries for help and rescue them.
You protect all those who love You,
    but You destroy the wicked.

I praise You, LORD, and may everyone on earth
    bless Your holy name forever and ever.

Your kingdom is an everlasting kingdom.
You rule throughout all generations.
You always keep Your promises.
You are gracious in all You do.
You help the fallen.
You satisfy the hunger and thirst of every living thing.
You are righteous in everything You do.
You are filled with kindness.
You are close to all who call on You in truth.
You hear the cries for help those who fear You.
You grant the desires of those who fear You.
You rescue those who fear You.
You protect those who love You.
You destroy the wicked.

146

I praise You, LORD!

Let all that I am praise You.
I will praise You as long as I live.
I will sing praises to You, my God, with my dying breath.
I will not put my confidence in powerful people;
    There is no help for me there.
When they breathe their last, they return to the earth,
    and all their plans die with them.

But I am joyful because I have You,
    the God of Israel, as my helper.
My hope is in You, my God.

You made heaven and earth,
    the sea, and everything in them.
You keep every promise forever.
You give justice to the oppressed
    and food to the hungry.
You free the prisoners.
You open the eyes of the blind.

You are my hope.
You made heaven and earth.
You keep every promise forever.
You give justice to the oppressed.
You give food to the hungry.
You free the prisoners.
You open the eyes of the blind.

You lift up those who are weighed down.
You love the godly.
You protect the foreigners around me.
You care for the orphans and widows,
    but You frustrate the plans of the wicked.

You will reign forever.
You will be my God.

I praise You, LORD!

> *You lift up those who are weighed down.*
> *You love the godly.*
> *You protect the foreigners around me.*
> *You care for orphans and widows.*
> *You frustrate the plans of the wicked.*
> *You will reign forever.*
> *You are my God.*

147

I praise You, LORD!

How good to sing praises to You, my God!
How delightful and how fitting!
You are rebuilding Jerusalem
  and bringing the exiles back to Israel.
You heal the brokenhearted and bandage their wounds.
You count the stars and call them all by name.

How great are You, Lord! Your power is absolute!
Your understanding is beyond comprehension!
You support the humble,
  but You bring the wicked down into the dust.
I sing out my thanks to You, LORD;
  I sing praises to You, my God.

You cover the heavens with clouds, provide rain for the earth,
  and make the grass grow in mountain pastures.
You give food to the wild animals
  and feed the young ravens when they cry.
You take no pleasure in the strength of a horse
  or in human might.
No, Your delight is in those who fear You,
  those who put their hope in Your unfailing love.
I will glorify You, LORD.
I will praise You, my God.

> *You heal the brokenhearted.*
> *Your power is absolute.*
> *Your understanding is beyond comprehension.*
> *You support the humble.*
> *You bring the wicked down into the dust.*
> *You provide for the earth.*
> *You delight in those who fear You.*

For You have strengthened the bars of my gates
    and blessed the children within my walls.
You send peace across my nation
    and satisfy my hunger with the finest wheat.
You send Your orders to the world—
    how swiftly Your word flies!
You send the snow like white wool;
    You scatter frost upon the ground like ashes.
You hurl the hail like stones.
Who can stand against Your freezing cold?
Then, at Your command, it all melts.
You send Your winds, and the ice thaws.

You have revealed Your words to Jacob,
    Your decrees and regulations to Israel.
You have not done this for any other nation;
    They do not know Your regulations.

I praise You LORD!

Your love is unfailing.
You send peace.
You satisfy my hunger.

148

I praise You, LORD!

May the heavens praise You.
May the skies praise You.
May all angels praise You.
May all the armies of heaven praise You.
May the sun and moon praise You.
May all twinkling stars praise You.
May the skies above praise You.
May the vapors high above the clouds praise You.
May every created thing give praise to You, LORD,
    for You issued Your command, and they came into being.

You established them forever and ever.
Your decree will never be revoked.

May the creatures of the ocean depths
    praise You from the earth.

Fire and hail, snow and clouds,
    wind and weather that obey You,
    mountains and all hills,
    fruit trees and all cedars,
    wild animals and all livestock,
    small scurrying animals and birds,
    kings of the earth and all people,
    rulers and judges of the earth,
    young men and young women,
    old men and children;
    May they all praise Your name.

You created everything.

For Your name is very great;
Your glory towers over the earth and heaven!

You have made Your people strong,
honoring Your faithful ones—
the people of Israel who are close to You.

I praise You, Lord!

Your name is very great.
You made me strong.

149

I praise You, LORD!

I will sing a new song to You.
I will sing Your praises in the assembly of the faithful.
I will rejoice in You, my Maker.
I will exult in You, my King.
I will praise Your name with dancing and music.

For You delight in Your people;
    You crown the humble with victory.
I will rejoice that You honor me.
I will sing for joy as I lie on my bed.

Your praises will be in my mouth,
    as it was with Your people long ago,
    who held a sharp sword in their hands—
    to execute vengeance on the nations
    and punishment on the peoples,
    to bind their kings with shackles
    and their leaders with iron chains,
    to execute the judgment written against them.

Such vindication is an honor for Your faithful ones.

I praise You, LORD!

You delight in Your people.
You crown the humble with victory.

150

I praise You, LORD!

I praise You in Your sanctuary.
I praise You in Your mighty heaven.
I praise You for Your mighty works.
I praise Your unequaled greatness.
I praise You with a blast of the ram's horn.
I praise You with the lyre and harp.
I praise You with the tambourine and dancing.
I praise You with strings and flutes.
I praise You with a clash of cymbals.
I praise You with loud clanging cymbals.

May everything that breathes sing praises to You, LORD!

I praise You, LORD!

Your greatness is unequaled.

You guard my way. You are mighty. You are sovereign. You are my refuge. You are a shield around me. You are my glory. You are the lifter of my head. You answer me when I cry out to You. You watch over me. You save me. You are my liberator. You hear me when I call. You give me joy. You are my protector. You take no pleasure in wickedness. You bless the godly. You answer my prayers. You judge the nations. You are my shield. You are just. You are majestic. You created everything. You reign forever. You care for the helpless. You are a shelter for the oppressed. You are just. You are alive. You see everything. You defend the orphans and the oppressed. You are King forever and ever. You rule from heaven. You are righteous. Your promises are pure. You will protect the oppressed. You love me. You saved me. You are good to me. You are with me. You are my protector. You are holy. You are my Lord. You are my inheritance. You are my ultimate joy. You see those who do right. You are my protector. You are my rock. You are my fortress. You are my savior. You are my shield. You are the power that saves me. You are my place of safety. You are worthy of praise. You have rescued me. You have rewarded me. Your way is perfect. Your promises prove true. You live. Your love is unfailing. You are the mighty Creator. Your law is perfect. Your testimony is sure. Your precepts are right. Your commandment is pure. Your laws are true. Your laws are sweeter than honey. Your laws are a warning. Your laws are a reward. You are my rock. You are my redeemer. You answer my prayers. Your name alone is powerful. You are all powerful. You are holy. You listen to the cries of the needy. You rule all the nations. You are my shepherd. You are with me. You are my inheritance. You are invincible in battle. You are the King of Glory. You are merciful. You are good. You do what is right. You are my friend. You rescue me. You are my hope. You are faithful. You are my light. You are my salvation. You are my fortress. You will never abandon me. You are just. You hear me. You are my strength. You help me. You fill my heart with joy. You are majestic. You are the Eternal King. You heal me. You turn my sorrow to joy. You are my refuge. You are my hope. You are my hiding place. You are my guide. You are Creator of all. You are my hope. You are my help. You are my shield. You are great. You answer me. You free me from all my fears. You rescue me from all my troubles. You are near to me when I am brokenhearted. You vindicate me. You are just. You are the fountain of life. Your love never fails. You give me the desires of my heart. You will destroy the wicked. You take care of the godly. You take care of the innocent. You direct the steps of the godly. You delight in every detail of my life. You hold me by the hand. You love justice. You will never abandon me. You will keep me safe forever. You will not let the wicked succeed. You will not let me be condemned. You will honor me. You will destroy the rebellious. You will rescue me. You are my fortress. You help me. You rescue me from the wicked. You save me. You are my shelter. You hear my every sigh. You are my Savior. You are my only hope. You discipline me. You turn to me. You hear my cries. You lift me out of despair. You give me a new song to sing. You have no equal. You take no delight in sacrifices. You are faithful. Your love is unfailing. You are great. You are my helper and my savior. You care for the poor. You are the Great Healer. You give me access to Your presence. You are worthy of all praise. You are alive. You are the Living Water. You are my Savior. You are my God. You give me life. You are my rock. You have not forgotten me. You are my Savior. You are my God. You are my only safe haven. You are the source of all my joy. You are my Savior. You are my God. You give me victory. You know the secrets of every heart. You are my King and my God. You are my Redeemer. You are the most handsome of all. You are a warrior.

You defend truth, humility, and justice. You love justice and hate evil. You will exalt me. You are worthy of all honor and praise forever and ever. You are my refuge and strength. You are here with me. You are my fortress. You are God. You will be exalted among the nations. You will be exalted in the earth. You are awesome. You rule the whole earth. You are great. You deserve all praise. Your love is unfailing. You are my God forever and ever. You are my guide. You are my Redeemer. You have power over the grave. You shine in glorious radiance. You will not remain silent. You need nothing. You will rescue me and honor me. You are justified when You speak. You are blameless when You judge. You will make me know wisdom. You do not delight in sacrifice. You are not pleased with burnt offering. You delight in a broken spirit and a contrite heart. Your justice continues forever. Your love is unfailing. You will scatter the bones of Your enemies. You brought salvation out of Jerusalem. You are my helper. You keep me alive. Your name is good. You have rescued me. You will rescue me. You hear my voice. You ransom me and keep me safe. You have ruled forever. You will take care of me. You will not permit the godly to slip and fall. You will save me. You are for me. You keep Your promises. You have delivered my soul from death. You keep my feet from stumbling. You are worthy of all my trust. You will save me from my enemies. You are worthy of all praise. You will judge the earth. You will bring justice. You scoff at all the hostile nations. You are my strength, my fortress, and my refuge. You will rescue me. You will stand with me. You are my strength. You show me unfailing love. You will lead me. You will never reject me. You will enable me to do mighty things. You are my rock. You are my safe refuge. You are a fortress, protecting me from my enemies. You have given me an inheritance of eternity with You. You alone are my rock and my salvation. You are my fortress. You are my refuge. You repay all people according to what they have done. You are my God. Your unfailing love is better than life itself. You hold me securely. You hear my complaints. You will destroy my enemies. You protect me. You answer my prayers. You forgive my sins. You are my savior. You are the hope of everyone on earth. You formed the mountains by Your power. You inspire shouts of joy. You take care of the earth. Your deeds are awesome. You keep my feet from stumbling. You have purified me like silver. You pay attention to my prayers. You love me perpetually. You govern the nations with justice. You bless me. Your name is the LORD. You set the prisoners free. You are my Savior. You carry me in Your arms. You rescue me from death. You are the source of life. You give power and strength to Your people. You know me. You give me faith. Your love is unfailing. Your salvation is sure. Your unfailing love is wonderful. Your mercy is plentiful. You are my rescuer. You hear the cries of the needy. You are my helper. You are my savior. You do what is right. You are my rock and my fortress. You alone are my hope. You have cared for me from birth. You alone are just. You will restore me. You are faithful to Your promises. You have ransomed me. Your Son will rule all. You defend the poor. You rescue the children of the needy. You crush the oppressor. Your name will endure forever. You will judge the wicked. You are my guide. You are my heart's desire. You are my refuge. Your name is great. You are resplendent. You judge those who do evil. You are to be feared. You break the spirit of rulers. Your ways are holy. You are the God of great wonders. You redeem Your people. You've done great and miraculous things throughout history. You are patient, not wanting any to perish but for all to come to repentance. You lead Your people. You are enthroned above the cherubim. You are the God of heaven's armies. You are my only means of salvation. You are my strength. You are the giver of good things. You rule over everything.

You care for the poor and the orphan. You avenge Your people. You alone are the LORD Most High. You are the living God. You are my King and my God. You are my sun and shield. You give me grace and glory. You give me good things. You speak peace to me. You pour down Your blessings on me. You are my God. You are so good. You are so ready to forgive. You are great and perform wonderful deeds. You alone are God. Your love for me is very great. You have rescued me. You are a God of compassion and mercy. You are slow to get angry. You are filled with unfailing love and faithfulness. You love Jerusalem. You are the source of all joy. You are the God of my salvation. Your unfailing love will last forever. You are entirely faithful. You created everything. You make me strong. You protect me. You cannot lie. You promise Your unfailing love. You are God. You see all my secret sins. Your love is unfailing. You alone are my refuge, my place of safety. You hear me when I call. You are my salvation. Your love is unfailing. You are forever faithful. You do great works. You are just. You are my rock. You are King. You are robed in majesty. You are eternal. You are mightier than the violent raging of the seas. You are mightier than the breakers on the shore. You are holy. You know people's thoughts. You will not abandon Your people. You are my fortress. You are the mighty rock. You will destroy evil people. You are a great God. You are a great King, above all gods. You made the sea and the dry land. You made me and watch over me. You speak to me. You welcome me into Your place of rest. You save. You are great. You are worthy of praise. You are to be feared. You made the heavens. You deserve all glory. You reign. You will judge everyone fairly. You are coming to judge the earth. You reign. You are supreme over all the earth. You protect the lives of Your faithful followers. You have done wonderful things. You have made known Your salvation. You have revealed Your righteousness to every nation. You are coming to judge the world with justice and fairness. You are my king. Your name is holy. You are holy. You are God. You made me. You are good. Your love and Your faithfulness endure forever. You deserve my praise and my full devotion. You will sit on Your throne forever. You will appear in Your glory. You live forever. You laid the foundation of the earth. You forgive all my sins. You fill my life with good things. You are compassionate and gracious. You are slow to anger. You remove my transgressions from me. You rule over everything. You are great. You created everything. You maintain everything. You take pleasure in all You have made. You are great. You stand by Your covenant. You orchestrate everything. You brought Your people out of Egypt. You satisfied their hunger. You are good. You are so patient. You get angry when we turn from you. Your love is unfailing. You are good. You satisfy the thirsty soul. You are so powerful. Your love is great. You have done wonderful things. You rescue the poor from trouble. Your lovingkindness is great above the heavens. Your truth reaches to the skies. You will trample down my adversaries. You are worthy of praise. You are so faithful and good. You stand beside the needy. You stand ready to save. You give dominion to the King. Your deeds are amazing. Your righteousness never fails. You give food to those who fear You. You always remember Your covenant. You have paid my ransom in full. Your name is holy and awe-inspiring. You bless those who fear You and walk in Your way. You are high above the nations. Your glory is higher than the heavens. You are beyond comparison. You are enthroned on high. You care for the poor. Your presence causes the whole earth to tremble. You are worthy of all glory. You are my help and my shield. You will bless me. You hear me. You are kind. You are good. You are merciful. You protect those of childlike faith. You have been good to me. You have saved me from death. You have freed me from my chains.

Your unfailing love for me is powerful. Your faithfulness endures forever. You are good. Your love endures forever. You answer me and set me free. You are for me, and You will help me. You are my strength and my song. You give me victory. You are the creator of each day. You are my God. You are good. Your love endures forever. Your Word is good. You answer my prayer. You will punish the wicked. You made heaven and earth. You will not let me stumble. You watch over me. You never sleep. You stand beside me. You keep me from all harm. You keep watch over me. You love Jerusalem. You are enthroned in heaven. You give mercy. You are on my side. You made heaven and earth. You surround me. You do amazing things for me. You are my provider. You bless those who fear You. You are good. You keep no record of my sins. You offer forgiveness. You love me with unfailing love. Your redemption overflows. You are my hope. You make eternal promises. You give eternal life. You are praiseworthy. You made heaven and earth. You are praiseworthy. You are good. You are greater than any other god. You do whatever You please. Your name endures forever. You will give justice to Your people. You will have compassion on Your servants. You are good. You alone do mighty miracles. You made the heavens. You brought Israel out of Egypt. Your faithful love endures forever. You remembered me in my weakness. You saved me from my enemies. You give food to every living thing. Your faithful love endures forever. You will execute justice. Your love is unfailing. Your promises are backed by Your name. You answer me. You encourage me. You give me strength. Your glory is very great. You are great. You care for the humble. You keep Your distance from the proud. You will protect me. You will work out Your plans for my life. Your love endures forever. You made me. You know me. You understand my thoughts. You are intimately acquainted with all my ways. You know everything. You are everywhere. You created me with great care. You control everything. You are my God. You protect me. You give justice to the poor. You are my refuge. You alone know my path. You are my place of refuge. You are good to me. You are faithful and righteous. Your love is unfailing. You are my God. Your Spirit leads me. You are my ally, my fortress, and my tower of safety. You are my rescuer, my shield, and my refuge. You give joy. You are great. You are most worthy of praise. You are merciful and compassionate. You are slow to get angry. You are filled with unfailing love. You are good to everyone. You shower compassion on all Your creation. Your kingdom is an everlasting kingdom. You rule throughout all generations. You always keep Your promises. You are gracious in all You do. You help the fallen. You satisfy the hunger and thirst of every living thing. You are righteous in everything You do. You are filled with kindness. You are close to all who call on You in truth. You hear the cries for help those who fear You. You grant the desires of those who fear You. You rescue those who fear You. You protect those who love You. You destroy the wicked. You are my hope. You made heaven and earth. You keep every promise forever. You give justice to the oppressed. You give food to the hungry. You free the prisoners. You open the eyes of the blind. You lift up those who are weighed down. You love the godly. You protect the foreigners around me. You care for orphans and widows. You frustrate the plans of the wicked. You will reign forever. You are my God. You heal the brokenhearted. Your power is absolute. Your understanding is beyond comprehension. You support the humble. You bring the wicked down into the dust. You provide for the earth. You delight in those who fear You. Your love is unfailing. You send peace. You satisfy my hunger. You created everything. Your name is very great. Your name is very great. You delight in Your people. You crown the humble with victory. Your greatness is unequaled.

Printed in the United States
by Baker & Taylor Publisher Services